N. G. Carraway paints an intimate and fascinating portrait of a shepherd boy's life, during the period a few years before, and after, the birth of Jesus. The reader experiences the events of young Josiah's life, the shepherd's work, their land and culture, with astonishing realism and immediacy. Using the biblical narratives in the synoptic gospels, this is both compelling drama and scholarly teaching—for both Jew and Gentile. With provocative questions and comments at the end of each chapter, the author carefully guides the reader through the inherent theology of prophecy and salvation. Revealing the Jewish roots of Christianity, and the universal need for a Savior, this book should be read by people of all faiths.

Bob McGuire,
Playwright, dramatist, actor

"Trust in the Lord with all your heart, and lean not on your own understanding; In all your ways acknowledge Him, and He shall direct your paths." (Proverbs 3:5-6, New King James Version)

Shalom,

JOURNEY
on the
ANCIENT PATH

The Way of the Shepherd

*Are you desperate to know
a living God who loves you?
Journey the ancient path
to discover the heart of the One
who created you!*

N. G. Carraway

N. G. CARRAWAY

XULON PRESS

Xulon Press
2301 Lucien Way #415
Maitland, FL 32751
407.339.4217
www.xulonpress.com

Visit the author's website at https://ngcarraway.com

Unless otherwise indicated, Scripture quotations taken from the English Standard Version (ESV). Copyright © 2001 by Crossway, a publishing ministry of Good News Publishers. Used by permission. All rights reserved.

Paperback ISBN-13: 978-1-6628-3160-7
Ebook ISBN-13: 978-1-6628-3161-4

Dedication

This book is dedicated to my friend, Sonam Tripathy, who now lives in India, and to all the other readers in the world who do not yet know the story of the most amazing man every born. His name is Yeshua (Jesus) and over 2,000 years ago, he changed the course of history. Because of his life and ministry, time as we know it, was split in half.

The most compelling evidence for an eternal, all-knowing God, is the ability to accurately foretell future events. There are over a hundred prophecies recorded in the Tanakh (Old Testament of the Holy Bible), about a Messiah who would come to earth, to save the people of the world. Most of these prophecies were accurately fulfilled during the life of Jesus, as recorded in the New Testament of the Holy Bible. There were many other prophecies spoken thousands of years ago, about Israel and the Jewish people, which were not fulfilled until the past few decades. And there are other prophecies still to be fulfilled.

This book is dedicated to you, the reader. May you read the words in this book and experience the "ruach elohim" (the spirit of God) in a personal and profound way. As you read this book, you will travel the ancient path foretold in the prophecies concerning the Jewish Messiah, and you will find hope. Before you read this book, simply say this sincere prayer; "God, if you are real, please reveal yourself to me".

Small Menorah

In many ways, the Jewish people are the spiritual 'fathers' of the Christians. And the Christians are the spiritual 'children' of the Jewish people. May we all walk in truth and become children of the light.

"Behold...before the great and awesome day of the Lord comes...he will turn the hearts of the fathers to their children and the hearts of children to their fathers." (Malachi 4:5, 6)

Table of Contents

Acknowledgements

S pecial acknowledgements are in order for a few individuals, who were instrumental in bringing this manuscript to completion or providing artwork. Susie Carraway, my granddaughter, is the artist who painted the beautiful menorah. Tracy Ratliff is the artist who painted the family of Mary, Joseph and Yeshua. Bob McGuire is a friend who encouraged me in the writing of this book and in learning Hebrew. And, my mom, Earlene Phillips, made a financial donation to help cover some of the expense of publishing this book. Other family members also encouraged me in this effort.

A special thanks goes to Julie Wilkerson, who coached me and encouraged me every step of the way. Since this was my first book, her knowledge of the publishing world was invaluable. She has been a constant source of encouragement and direction. Without her assistance, I am not sure this book would have been completed. All of these individuals had a part, in my effort to bring this book to you; and I am thankful for their help.

And finally, I must acknowledge the active participation, and involvement of the Holy Spirit, in writing this book. It was His prompting, in December of 2019, that I decided to undertake this task. While writing the various chapters, He would remind me of numerous sermons and teachings I had heard during my life. There are also several dreams detailed in this book. Every dream, written into the story line of this book, is a dream that I dreamed myself. One dream even included music! I believe these dreams where sent by the Holy Spirit, and for that, I am eternally grateful. The Holy Spirit has been my guide, my counsel and my encourager. I pray the Holy Spirit will invade your life with His presence. I pray that He will give you dreams and visions, which bring revelation and understanding about the God in heaven, who loves you with an everlasting love. He sent His only son, Jesus, to take the punishment of sin for all humanity, so that we can have eternal life with Him.

"And it shall come to pass afterward, that I will pour out my Spirit on all flesh; your sons and your daughters shall prophesy, your old men shall dream dreams, and your young men shall see visions." (Joel 2:28)

Introduction

The ancient Hebrew prophecies concerning the coming of the Savior of the world, the Messiah, are the foundation of this Biblical account. This novel follows a fictional shepherd boy, Josiah, who lived in Bethlehem 2,000 years ago. As Josiah sees the fulfillment of one prophecy after another, he is convinced that only God could orchestrate these events, hundreds of years *after* the prophecies were spoken.

Astonishing information, recently discovered in the Dead Sea Scrolls, is woven into this inspiring novel. Josiah's life becomes a journey of revelation, complete with angelic visitations and supernatural dreams. In keeping with Jewish tradition, Josiah's father teaches him about the importance of the annual Jewish feasts. These ancient feasts still have prophetic implications for us now, and in the future!

At the end of this book, there is a Prophecy Chart which lists all of the prophecies fulfilled when Jesus was born. This chart shows where the prophecy was spoken, in the Old Testament, and then fulfilled in the New Testament. There is also a Glossary at the back of the book with words which you may not know.

To truly understand the birth of Jesus, you must understand the context and the culture within which he was born. This book will endeavor to accomplish just that, by allowing you to see the birth of Jesus through the eyes of the shepherds, who lived in Bethlehem. As you read this book, you travel 2,000 years into the past. You are taken on a journey to discover the heart of God, and his captivating plan for humanity. At the end of each chapter, there are comments and questions which will provoke you to think about the narrative you just read. Based on the prophecies given and later fulfilled, you will see undeniable proof that the God of the Bible truly exists. And that God sent His only son as the Savior of the world. A second book, about the life and ministry of Jesus, is already planned and will follow the same family of shepherds as they interact with Jesus, thirty years after his birth. Once you know who Jesus is, you will understand why He came.

"You will know the truth and the truth will set you free."
(John 8:32)

Chapter 1
The Tower of the Flock

Over 2,000 years ago, in the land of Israel...

"Hurry, Josiah! Come quickly! It's time, and I don't want you to miss this," Samuel, the shepherd, shouted to his young son, his long, brown beard gently moving with the wind. Dropping his well-worn blanket, Josiah jumped up and started toward his father. However, his foot was ensnared in the blanket, and he fell, headfirst on the ground.

"Are you okay, Josiah?" Samuel asked. "Be more careful, or you will break a leg," he admonished.

"Yes, I am okay," mumbled Josiah, as he wiped the dirt off his face and brushed the debris off his arms. He was thankful he landed in dirt, not on the rocky ground. He limped to his father's side, a big knot already forming on his left leg.

They both stared at the pregnant ewe as she struggled to give birth. "This will be her firstborn lamb," Samuel said, sharing the basics of shepherding with his young son. "I asked Adonai for a *boy* lamb," Samuel said.

"But why, father? Why did you want this to be a boy instead of a girl?" Josiah asked.

"Great question!" Samuel answered with a smile. "Let's help her deliver this lamb... We can talk later. Put your hands here, and when the lamb comes out, get ready to catch him. I don't want him to get injured."

Trembling with excitement and a little fear, Josiah placed his hands near the sheep. Josiah's tender, smooth skin made a sharp contrast to his father's old, weatherworn, wrinkled skin. Soon, he was holding a newborn lamb. The little lamb was kicking, wriggling, and trying to make sounds.

"It's so little and so beautiful," said Josiah breathlessly. "Is it a boy or a girl?"

"Let's introduce the mama to her newborn lamb and watch for a second lamb," Samuel replied. "Then, we will take the first lamb and see if it's a boy or a girl."

Josiah placed the lamb gently on the ground, in front of the mother lamb. The mother lamb looked at her offspring and slowly began to lick the little lamb, removing all traces this living creature had once been inside her body.

Ewe and baby lamb

Then, she turned and walked a few steps away to deliver another lamb.

It was a beautiful spring day in the hills surrounding the town of Bethlehem. The warm breeze and the new shoots of grass made the hillside a place of comfort, as the sheep gave birth to new life.

Josiah, his older brother Jonathan, and their father, Samuel, were shepherds along with 15 or 20 other men from the Bethlehem area. In the spring, when it was time for the new lambs to be born, the shepherds brought their sheep to an ancient one-story stone building, which served as a watchtower for the shepherds. The building was called Migdal Eder, which means the Tower of the Flock. The stone tower was built on a small hill near the ancient path to Jerusalem, only five miles away. The watchtower served as a place where the shepherds could easily keep an eye on their sheep in the fields below. The watchtower was located on the outskirts of Bethlehem.

"Josiah, watch what I do and learn what it means to be a shepherd for the Most High. Bring those strips of cloth with you," Samuel instructed, as he lifted the newborn lamb into his arms.

Samuel carried the lamb to a nearby bowl of water and gently used a piece of cloth to wash the little lamb while he examined every part of its body. He looked at the stomach area first and with a twinkle in his eyes, triumphantly declared, "It's a boy. I asked for a boy, and G-d told me this *would be* a boy lamb."

"And Adonai, our G-d never lies," Samuel said confidently. Samuel gently felt the legs, the stomach, and the ears of the little lamb. His wool was completely white. The lamb patiently stared at Samuel with dark eyes. He seemed to understand this was an important inspection.

"He is perfect!" declared Samuel, "He has been chosen for Adonai, and we must protect him. We do not want him to be injured. Hand me those strips of cloths, and listen carefully, my son."

Josiah handed Samuel the strips of cloth, one at a time, and watched intently as Samuel began to snugly wrap the newborn lamb. Josiah had always been inquisitive. He was a thinker who constantly asked questions. He wanted to know *why* the shepherds did certain activities and *how* they knew the times and the seasons.

As Samuel wrapped the lamb, he began to speak. "A few months ago, you turned nine years old. However, you have been learning our Holy Scriptures since you were young. So you already know the story of how our people were slaves in Egypt for over four hundred years, until Adonai sent someone to deliver them."

"Yes, I know the story," Josiah replied. "Moses led our ancestors out of Egypt, where the Egyptians served many evil and false gods. The Egyptians did not obey the one, true G-d. Moses came to lead our people to the land of Israel."

"Yes, you are correct," Samuel replied. "On the night before they left Egypt, Adonai told us to kill a lamb, but not *any* lamb. It had to be a perfect, one-year-old, male lamb. This lamb would be cooked for a special dinner. And the blood of the innocent lamb was placed on the sides and the top of the door to the house where each family lived."

"Later in the evening," Samuel continued, "each family gathered to eat the roasted lamb, as they prepared to leave Egypt. That same night, an angel came to the land of Egypt. If the house did not have the lamb's blood on the door posts, the firstborn son died."

"But the angel *passed over* the houses of the children of our fore-fathers—the houses with the blood on the door posts. The firstborn son was spared in *those* homes, which is why we call this event Pesach, which means 'to pass over.'"

"We gained our freedom that night. G-d raised up Moses to be our savior. He delivered us from the evil world where we lived because we could not save ourselves. Now, we live in the land that G-d gave us. And each year, a perfect one-year-old male lamb is again sacrificed at Pesach, as a reminder of G-d's promise."

"My son, do not forget. Adonai, our G-d, *never* lies!"

"In a couple of weeks," Samuel continued, "we will celebrate Pesach. Your older brother Jonathan and I will travel to Jerusalem. You are too young to go this year. But next year, you will go with us to Jerusalem for Passover."

"Our rabbis say, 'All roads lead to Jerusalem.' And the road which leads to Jerusalem is an ancient path our ancestors walked, in their journey of faith."

Now, the lamb was wrapped in strips of cloth, swaddled like a baby, with only the lamb's head visible. "These strips of cloth have been given to us from the priests at the Temple," Samuel said. "They are made from garments which the priests have worn. When these garments become dirty or bloody from the animal sacrifices, they rip them into strips for us to use."

Samuel picked up the lamb, and said to Josiah, "Follow me." He turned and walked to the nearby stone building, with the lamb cradled in his arms. "This building is called the Tower of the Flock," Samuel explained as he pushed open the ancient door.

Inside the small building were several items that made the building livable. There was a bed in the corner, a couple of old chairs, a small table, and several bowls and pots. On the wall, there were several brackets where lanterns could be hung. There was a small fireplace in the corner. Someone had left several small branches and hay, in case a fire was needed. In the spring, the local shepherds would stay in this tower while the new lambs were being birthed.

Outside of the tower, steps led to the flat roof. Near the door of the tower, there was a stone feeding trough, called a manger. Samuel turned and pointed to the feeding trough.

"Do you see the feeding trough we use when feeding the animals?" he asked Josiah.

"Yes, I put hay in it when there is no grass outside for the sheep to eat," Josiah replied.

"Take this perfect little lamb, and place him in the manger," Samuel instructed Josiah.

He did as his father asked, tenderly placing the lamb in the feeding trough. Josiah gently stroked the top of the lamb's white, furry head. The newborn lamb closed his eyes, as if going to sleep.

Josiah thought the little lamb was the most beautiful creature he had ever seen. He imagined this little lamb would be his pet, his constant companion. Some of his older friends had lambs as pets, and he always wanted one for himself. His heart was bursting with affection for this little lamb. He smiled to himself and softly spoke to the lamb, "You are my best friend, and you don't even know it yet."

Samuel gently spoke and interrupted Josiah's thoughts. "This manger is the perfect place to keep our little lamb safe, while we help his mother deliver the rest of her babies today. We place a perfect male lamb in the manger, so we know he has been selected for the Passover sacrifice."

Josiah's head jerked up as tears began to roll down his cheeks. His lips quivered. He stared intently at his father, stuttering, "You mean, you, this lamb, you mean... ?"

Samuel placed his hand on his young son, slowly nodding his head. "Yes, my son, this little lamb must be taken next year to Jerusalem, along with many others, for the Passover sacrifice. Our family is one of several families which have the honor to provide the lambs for this important sacrifice to Adonai."

"The Levite priests have chosen the shepherds in *this* area to take care of these special sheep," Samuel instructed. "Our sheep are the only ones allowed to be used for the Passover sacrifice in the Temple. These lambs must be spotless and without blemish when they are sacrificed. They require special treatment, which we will provide for them. Our sheep are also used for two daily sacrifices at the Temple."

"Since the time of King David, our family has lived here in Bethlehem. We have raised the lambs for the Temple sacrifices. This is the way we make our living."

"Tonight," Samuel continued, "after dark, we will go to the top of the tower and light a torch, holding it up to the sky. With Jerusalem only a few miles away, the priests will see our light and know an acceptable lamb has been born — a lamb worthy to be slain."

"The shepherds in Bethlehem are the *only* shepherds who can certify a perfect, sacrificial lamb has been born for Passover. The swaddling clothes are how we distinguish between the consecrated and the common. The common sheep will be sold to other shepherds, while we keep all of the unblemished lambs to breed again and to take to Jerusalem as a sacrifice. This makes our flocks very valuable. This is an ancient practice which has been handed down for generations."

"But, father, why must a lamb be sacrificed *again*?" Josiah moaned. "Adonai delivered our people from slavery long ago, when the *first* lamb was killed, at the *first* Passover. Why must we kill a lamb *every year*? I don't understand," Josiah cried, shaking his head and rubbing his eyes to wipe away the tears.

"The Passover sacrifice reminds us Adonai delivered us from the bondage of wicked masters," Samuel replied. "Adonai has commanded this, whether we understand it or not."

"We are no longer slaves in Egypt. Now, in our own country, the wicked Roman rulers have taken control of our land. They treat us almost like slaves. Even some of our own people have turned away from G-d and have worshipped the Roman gods. We know there is only one G-d, and he is King of the Universe."

"In the beginning of creation, Adam and Eve listened to the serpent and sinned against G-d. As punishment, they were banished from the Garden of Eden, that beautiful and perfect garden."

"G-d promised a Messiah, a Savior, would be born, the offspring of a woman. G-d also promised the Messiah would crush the enemy, that evil serpent."[1]

---

[1] See prophecy 1 in the Prophecy Chart.

"Seven hundred years ago, the prophet Micah told us the Messiah would be born in Bethlehem, in the city where we live."[2]

"It has now been over four hundred years since Adonai spoke to one of our prophets—like the four hundred years which passed when our people were slaves in Egypt. Perhaps it is time for *our* Savior, the Messiah, to come to the people of Israel!" Samuel exclaimed.

"Now, go find your brother Jonathan. Ask him to come help me with the pregnant sheep. Your little lamb is safe," Samuel said.

As he rose to leave, Josiah hugged his little lamb one last time. He was heartbroken. He wiped his eyes again as he shook his head. "I *don't* understand," he murmured to himself. "This lamb is perfect. He does *not deserve* to die; it's not fair." Josiah slowly limped away, searching for Jonathan.

The other shepherds were nearby with their flocks. There were many pregnant sheep that might give birth at any moment. It would be a busy day at the tower of the flock. It was the way of the shepherd.

A few weeks later, Samuel and Josiah were walking toward the tower when it began to hail. The hailstones were raining down on their heads as they ran into the tower.

"Father, what is this?" Josiah asked. "It's raining rocks from the sky!"

"No, it is hail," Samuel laughed. "Catch some in this pot, and I will show you a mystery."

Josiah took the pot and went outside, not exactly sure what his father had planned. When the pot was half full, he ran back inside the tower and put the pot on the table.

"We don't get hail very often; it's the first time you have seen hail," said Samuel. "As I talk, watch what happens to the hail. You know G-d created the universe and everything in it. He made the seas and the land. And he makes rain fall from the sky."

Samuel continued talking for several minutes. As Josiah watched the hailstones, to his amazement, they melted and turned into water.

---

[2] See prophecy 2 in the Prophecy Chart.

"It is a mystery, but G-d can take rain and turn it into icy stones which fall from the sky. This usually happens in the springtime. You have never seen snow either. When it melts, it becomes water. All three things are the same—they are water. Nevertheless, they fall from the sky in a different form. One element that can take three different forms. Three in one; one which can be experienced in three different forms."

Josiah was stunned. How could one thing have three different forms? But he knew it was true, he saw the hail melt and become water.

"It has stopped hailing. Let's go check on the sheep," Samuel said, and they left the tower.

Josiah had now seen hail, but he had never seen snow, which was rare for Bethlehem. Jonathan told him the last time it snowed was right before Josiah was born. He hoped one year it would snow again, so he could see another aspect of this mystery for himself.

Journey on the Ancient Path - The Way of the Shepherd
Chapter 1 - The Tower of the Flock

Thought Provoking Journey:

- In Biblical times, only the Levitical shepherds in Bethlehem, could certify a lamb as one worthy to be used for the Passover sacrifice.

- The Messiah had to be born in Bethlehem to fulfill a very specific prophecy, spoken centuries earlier. Would the Messiah be born in Bethlehem so he could also be certified (as the Lamb of God) by the Levitical shepherds?

- Was there a prophetic reason for a torch to be displayed at night, on the rooftop of the tower, when a Passover lamb was born? Did it foreshadow something that would happen when the Messiah would be born?

- There was a span of about 400 years between the last prophet Malachi, of the Tanakh (Old Testament), until Yeshua was born. These are sometimes called the 'silent years'. But was God truly silent? Are there any ancient accounts, such as the Dead Sea Scrolls, which might provide a historical record for those 400 years?

- The Hebrew word for water is 'mayim' and its form is plural. Why is this a plural word? Maybe it is because water has different forms? Also, when the flood occurred, the Scriptures mention the 'waters above and the waters below'.

Chapter 1 Thoughts

Chapter 2
Everlasting Covenant

<.. ———— ०✦० ———— ..>

Several weeks later...

"Josiah, wake up. We will be leaving soon," Samuel joyfully said, as he gently tugged at Josiah's leg. "We must get ready to go up to Jerusalem for your brother's betrothal ceremony."

Josiah rubbed the sleep out of his eyes and jumped out of bed, remembering the conversation with his father last night. "It's not too far. It will only take about three hours to walk to Jerusalem," Samuel had explained to Josiah before he went to bed. Jonathan was to complete the betrothal ceremony today. It was Josiah's first trip to Jerusalem, the Holy City.

Their father had arranged with another Jewish family for Jonathan to marry their daughter, a young woman named Rachel, who lived in Jerusalem. This arrangement was made when the children were very young. Tonight, at sundown, the celebration of Shavuot, also called the Feast of Weeks, would begin. All devout Jewish men would be in Jerusalem, as required by the Jewish Law. It was also a custom for a couple to become betrothed during this Feast.

Within a few minutes, Josiah, his mother, his father Samuel, his sister and his brother Jonathan, were ready to begin the six-mile trek to Jerusalem. Their donkey was packed with food and water for the trip and special gifts for the bride and her family. Josiah could only imagine the dancing, the singing, and the food he would eat tonight.

It appeared the whole village was traveling from Bethlehem to Jerusalem, to celebrate the Feast of Weeks. Josiah's family brought one of their best lambs to sacrifice as worship at the Temple. It was a way to say, "Thank you, Adonai, for this blessing." They also brought wine and other food for the betrothal celebration. As they walked, Samuel began to explain to Josiah the importance of what would take place later that day.

"Josiah," Samuel began, "I want to tell you a love story."

"Yes, Father, tell me the story of Jonathan and Rachel," Josiah exclaimed, his eyes wide open with excitement.

"Well, before you hear *their* love story, you must hear about the *first* love story—the greatest love story ever told!"

"What do you mean, the *greatest* love story?" Josiah looked intently into his father's eyes.

"This story was written over a thousand years ago, and it tells the story of how G-d, who created the universe and everything in it, how he loved his creation *so much,* he made a marriage contract with our ancestors."

"What?" Josiah was amazed. "What do you mean... a *marriage contract* with G-d?"

"There are three steps in the marriage process for our people. The first step is the selection of the bride. This is done by the two fathers. Afterwards, the bride's family enters into an agreement with the groom's family. The fathers perform this when the bride and groom are very young. They may not even know each other at this time.

"The betrothal is the second step. This is where the couple stands under a special canopy and they make a covenant with each other and with Adonai. They promise to cling to one another as if they are one. They both sign a document that is legally binding. The groom must also pay the 'bride price' to the bride's father. She will use this money to buy fabric for her dress and other items she may need for the wedding. This money is also given to the bride in case the groom cannot complete the wedding for some reason.

"The third and final step is the wedding, which takes place *after* the groom has prepared a place to live, for his wife and their children. This has been the custom among our people for many generations. It is both a solemn and joyful occasion.

"But the *first* and greatest love story is this: G-d, our Heavenly Father, chose Abraham to begin a new kind of family. G-d promised Abraham this 'marriage' covenant would result in a blessing to *all* the people on the earth, not just a blessing to Abraham's descendants.

"Therefore, the first step was the selection of a people group: the Jewish people, a 'bride' for Adonai. G-d chose the Jewish people through which He would seal His Covenant; those who are the descendants of Jacob's twelve sons through the lineage of Abraham, Isaac, and Jacob.

"The 'betrothal' between G-d and our people took place after our ancestors left Egypt. Moses led the children of Israel to Mount Sinai and the journey took fifty days. Then, G-d came down on the mountain in a thick cloud in the sight of all the people. This is when G-d gave the Ten Commandments and the Torah to the people, through Moses.

"The Torah is the contract, an ancient Covenant between G-d and man. The Jewish people have been the ones to preserve the Torah teachings for over a thousand years.

"Did you know the clouds of glory on Mount Sinai represented Heaven, which is the home of the bridegroom, Adonai? That is why during the betrothal ceremony, the couple stands under a chuppah, a white canopy, to remember the clouds of glory at Mount Sinai. This signifies a marriage has been made in heaven."

Josiah, with an astonished look, moved closer to his father as he continued. "G-d even told Moses to create the Ark of the Covenant so the Ten Commandments could be stored inside. The Ten Commandments tell us how to live, as the bride of G-d, and how we should treat each other."

"Finally, the third step was when our ancestors entered the Promised Land, the land our bridegroom, Adonai, had prepared for us. We were set apart for Adonai as His bride, His people, and His holy nation. Even in the wilderness, when G-d ordered the tabernacle to be built, it was called the Tent of Meeting because G-d came down to meet with mankind there. G-d wanted to live in the midst of His beloved bride, the children of Israel.

"So *this* feast, Shavuot, is fifty days *after* Passover and is remembered as a day of covenant.[3] In fact, our sages teach on *this* day G-d made a covenant with Noah after the flood. G-d gave the rainbow as a covenant sign that he would never flood the earth again. During this feast, we remember when G-d made an everlasting covenant with our people at Mount Sinai.

"But Shavuot is also a day which our children may choose to become betrothed, under the canopy, and make a covenant of marriage. In addition, Jonathan will give special gifts to Rachel during the betrothal ceremony. His gift will be a sign of his love for her and his promise to come back and get her."

Josiah listened intently with wide-open eyes. "Father, you have already arranged for me to marry Abigail; that is the first part, correct?"

"Yes, my son, I have chosen Abigail as your wife, and her father agrees. Abigail's family is righteous, and her father is a rabbi. We believe she will make a godly wife for you." Samuel placed his hand on Josiah's shoulder. "Look, we are almost at the city gates of Jerusalem."

Josiah turned to see a massive stone wall in the distance. It surrounded the entire city of Jerusalem. A huge wooden gate stood wide

---

[3] Shavuot is also called Pentecost, or Feast of Weeks, in English.

open to welcome the thousands of visitors streaming toward the city. He could now see the Temple Mount and the white retaining wall built around the Temple complex. Above the wall, he could see part of the Glorious Temple. He blinked his eyes, trying to focus. The massive, white retaining wall shone brightly in the sunshine. For a minute, he thought the hill was covered with snow. Rays of sunshine reflected off the golden sides of the Temple in fiery splendor. Josiah gasped; it was a stunning sight!

"When a person gazes at the Temple for the first time, they cannot help but be overwhelmed with the beauty of this amazing structure," Samuel remarked. "Wait until you see the Temple up close. It is even more majestic and awe-inspiring."

His family passed through the city gate as Samuel led the way.

"This is the Essene Gate," Samuel explained. "We will stay in the Essene Quarters tonight."

Josiah was in Jerusalem. Since this was one of the three pilgrimage feasts, thousands of devout Jewish men, women, and children were traveling to Jerusalem. The streets were packed with travelers, donkeys, and camels coming from all over the countryside. Josiah had never seen so many people in one place at one time.

A group of Roman soldiers on horseback rode up behind them. With swords and whips in hand, they shouted, "Move out of the way!" Jonathan had stopped to give money to a group of beggars. As Jonathan maneuvered around the beggars, he accidentally stepped into the path of the soldiers, and they almost knocked him down. As the horses pushed past, Jonathan shoved his fist in the air and glared at the soldiers. Samuel grabbed Jonathan's arm and quickly led everyone to an inn, not far from Rachel's home. They could rest here until the betrothal ceremony took place, the following morning.

After dinner, Samuel led the family in the ancient Shema prayer. He turned to Josiah and announced, "Tomorrow morning, Jonathan and I will meet with Rachel's father. We must review the original terms of the betrothal contract and reach an agreement with Rachel's father. You will come with us, so you can learn about this process. But now, it is time to sleep."

Josiah made his way to bed and pondered the events of the day. He had never seen Jonathan angry before, and it startled him. Jerusalem was not a safe city like his beloved hometown of Bethlehem. He thought about the love story his father had shared on their trip. He knew the Jews were G-d's chosen people. But, he did *not* know until today, that G-d who lived in Heaven, actually *loved* the Jewish people with an everlasting love. However, he questioned why G-d allowed the Jews to be mistreated. Moreover, why did He allow their country to be occupied by the evil Roman forces? If G-d loves the Jewish people, why does G-d allow such evil to happen to them? He decided he would ask his father to explain.

As Josiah fell asleep, he recited the Shema prayer again. "Hear O Israel: The Lord our G-d, the Lord is one. You shall love the Lord your G-d with all your heart and with all your soul and with all your might," (Deuteronomy 6:4–5). As he softly quoted the ancient scriptures, he felt like a blanket of love had been wrapped around him, and he slept in perfect peace.

The following morning, after breakfast, Samuel, Jonathan, and Josiah met with Rachel's father to discuss the details of the arrangement. They wrote the details of the marriage covenant in a document called a Ketubah.

In the Ketubah, Jonathan agreed to protect Rachel, his wife, and to never harm her in any way. He agreed to perform the duties of a husband and to have children with her. Having children was an important function of being a good Jewish wife.

Jonathan also agreed any children born to them would be raised according to the laws of the Torah. Jonathan agreed to provide a safe and comfortable home for his bride and their family. This 'home' would be a room built as an addition to his father's house. He also agreed to pay the bride price of 50 shekels of silver to Rachel's father.

In the Ketubah, Rachel's father agreed when Jonathan returned to get Rachel, she would be allowed to leave her home to go live with the groom and his family.

The Ketubah also stated Rachel would serve her husband as a faithful wife and to have children with him. Rachel's father agreed to bless Rachel with a portion of his belongings so she could take those possessions with her to her new home. Moreover, since Rachel's father was a kind and generous man, he agreed any money left over, from the 50 shekels of silver, would also be given *back* to Rachel when Jonathan came to get her.

The Ketubah was the written contract, the agreement, between the two families. After the bride and groom signed the Ketubah, it was registered with the local Jewish administration. It was then legally binding on both parties.

After the men had completed the arrangements, Rachel's father took the Ketubah back to his house to show Rachel. Before the betrothal could take place, Rachel had to agree to the details in the Ketubah. She would *not* be forced to marry Jonathan; it was *her* decision.

The men returned to the inn. Samuel found the lamb that had been brought for the sacrifice. "Jonathan, let us go to the Temple," Samuel said, "It is time for you to offer a sacrifice to Adonai for His blessing on your betrothal. Josiah, you stay here with the family; we will return soon."

Josiah watched his father and brother leave, wishing he were old enough to go to the Temple with them. "Next year, father said I can go to the Temple," he thought to himself.

Meanwhile, the family members at the inn prepared for the betrothal ceremony, which would take place later that evening. A few hours later, Samuel and Jonathan returned and prepared for the ceremony. The entire family was now dressed in their best clothes and jewelry. Together, they walked the short distance to Rachel's house.

As they walked, Samuel turned to Josiah and explained the next step. "When we arrive at Rachel's house, Jonathan will stand at the door and knock. If Rachel opens the door, we will know she has agreed to the terms of the Ketubah, the covenant. She will let us into her home and the betrothal ceremony can take place. However, if she does *not* open the door, this means she does *not* agree with the terms of the contract or does not want to marry Jonathan. She has free will. The decision is hers to make," Samuel explained.

When they reached Rachel's house, Jonathan knocked loudly on the door and gently bowed his head, as if in prayer. Josiah saw the excitement and concern on his brother's face as he followed the ancient traditions. Would Rachel open the door to Jonathan's knock?

Jonathan did not have to wait long for Rachel's answer. The door was flung open wide, and Rachel stood in the doorway, smiling shyly and adorned in a beautiful, floor-length tunic. It was white and tied with a blue sash around her waist. Rachel looked radiant!

Jonathan turned around and grinned at his family, waiting behind him, as if to say, "She has accepted the Ketubah. And she accepted me as her husband."

As they stepped into Rachel's house, Josiah could feel the joy and excitement between these two young people, who knew since childhood they were destined for each other.

After the initial greetings between the two families, Rachel's father led them outside. Rachel and Jonathan's chuppah was decorated with white fabric and fragrant flowers. A table was placed under the chuppah. The Ketubah and a glass of wine were visible on the table.

When everyone was ready for the formal betrothal ceremony to begin, Jonathan and Rachel took their place under the chuppah, along with their fathers. Rachel's father held up the Ketubah and looked at Rachel. He asked, "Rachel, do you agree to this covenant with Jonathan, and will you become his bride and be faithful to him forever?"

"Yes, I agree," Rachel replied.

Next, Samuel held up the Ketubah and asked Jonathan, "Jonathan, do you agree to this covenant with Rachel? And will you become her groom and be faithful to her forever?"

Jonathan said, "Yes, I agree."

Samuel handed the Ketubah to Jonathan and Rachel for them to both sign, which they did. Jonathan turned to his friends and motioned for them to bring the gifts forward. He unfolded a beautiful white robe made of linen and silk, decorated with golden embroidery around the edges.

Jonathan said to Rachel, "I give you this robe so you will remember me while I prepare a place for us to live." He placed the robe on her shoulders. Next, he took a golden ring and declared, "I give you this ring as a reminder of my everlasting covenant with you. You will wear this ring as a reminder that you are now set apart for me. I am yours, and you are mine."

Jonathan gave several other gifts to Rachel, saying, "These gifts will serve as my promise I *will return* to get you." Both families then walked to a room where the covenant meal had been prepared. Together, they celebrated the new bride and groom.

Jonathan and Rachel were now considered legally betrothed to each other. But they would not live together until Jonathan came back to get Rachel for the wedding ceremony, which would take place at his house.

After the meal, the wine from under the chuppah was brought to the father of the groom. Samuel stood up and prayed a blessing over it, "Blessed are you, Lord our G-d, King of the Universe, who created the fruit of the vine." The cup of wine was passed to both Rachel and Jonathan. They each took a sip of the wine to seal the covenant.

The betrothal ceremony was finished. It was now time for music and dancing. One man was playing a lyre while other men played flutes, tambourines, and various instruments. Hannah, Josiah's younger sister, walked up to the man with the lyre and tried to touch the strings. Everyone laughed while her mother quickly picked her up, trying to distract her. Children loved the music, and even young children would sway or bounce to the rhythm of the song. It was amusing to watch.

Finally, it was time for Samuel and his family to leave and return to the inn. Tomorrow, they would travel back to Bethlehem. As everyone prepared to leave, Jonathan turned to Rachel and said, "I go to prepare a place for you. You will not see me face-to-face again until I come and take you to the place I prepare for you. However, during this time, my friend will come to you and bring messages from me. You can trust my friend."

Jonathan motioned to his friend David and said, "If David tells you anything, you will know it came from me. He will tell you what pleases me so you can learn more about me and prepare for our life together."

The two families said good night to each other and Samuel's family left. As they walked back to the inn, Samuel turned to Josiah. "Did you see Jonathan sign the Ketubah tonight?"

"Yes," Josiah answered, "I saw Jonathan sign the document."

"Do you know how G-d signed the marriage contract with our people, at Mount Sinai?" Samuel asked. Josiah shook his head.

"G-d came down from Heaven and wrote the Ten Commandments on two tablets of stone with His finger. *That was G-d's signature!* Never before or since has G-d done such a thing. The Ten Commandments are the marriage contract, a Covenant, between G-d and humanity."

Josiah was amazed. He had never heard it explained that way. "The Ten Commandments are much more than rules that we should follow," Samuel explained. "They represent a Covenant made between G-d, the Bridegroom, and us, his beloved Bride. The Covenant proves how much Adonai loves us. If everyone kept the Ten Commandments, life would be good and pleasant *for everyone,* as G-d intended. But when men break G-d's law, evil and wickedness are the result.

"Josiah, can you recite the Ten Commandments?" Samuel inquired.

"Yes, father," Josiah affirmed and immediately began to quote the ancient commandments.

> "You shall have no other gods before me.
> You shall not make any carved image of me.
> You shall not take the name of the Lord, your G-d, in vain.
> Remember the Sabbath day, to keep it holy.

Honor your father and your mother.

You shall not murder.

You shall not commit adultery.

You shall not steal.

You shall not bear false witness against your neighbor.

You shall not covet."

"Josiah, you are indeed a great student. You have learned much in your young life because you have a heart for the things of G-d, as King David did. Now, time for bed; we return to Bethlehem tomorrow."

Josiah thought his heart would burst. "Yes, I want to be like David. I want to be a man after G-d's own heart. It is the way of the shepherd," he thought to himself as he settled into his bed. He thought about the music everyone enjoyed tonight and how King David played a lyre as a young boy.

The day had been exciting but very long and tiring. In his mind, he could see the beautiful, white chuppah. He softly said the Shema prayer and then, he added his own prayer, "Adonai, show me how I can love you with everything I have. And is there any way I can get a lyre and learn how to play and sing like David did?" As he fell asleep, he thought he heard beautiful, heavenly music. In his mind's eye, he saw the white canopy from the betrothal ceremony, and it slowly became white clouds of glory. He drifted into a deep sleep, enveloped in a cloud of heavenly peace and love.

Thought Provoking Journey:

- God chose to use His feasts as types and shadows for future, important events. Some feasts foreshadow multiple events and some feasts point to events yet to come. For example, Pentecost (Shavuot, also known as the Feast of Oaths) represents a Covenant.

- According to Jewish tradition, Noah's rainbow appeared on this day (the Feast of Shavuot/Pentecost) to confirm God's covenant to never destroy the earth by a flood again.

- God came down on Mt. Sinai on this day (the Feast of Shavuot/Pentecost) and made an everlasting covenant with the Jewish people. This is known as the Covenant of the Law or the Covenant of the Torah.

- The Holy Spirit was poured out on the disciples in the upper room on this day (the Feast of Shavuot/Pentecost). God made a covenant with the New Testament church; this covenant became known as the Covenant of Grace.

- When God makes a covenant, it is everlasting on His part. But, the covenant may come with conditions; for example, Israel must be a faithful bride.

- The Ten Commandments are found in the Bible, in Exodus 20. Hundreds of years ago, these ten rules became the basis for the legal framework implemented in the United States and other parts of the world.

www.ngcarraway.com

Chapter 2 Thoughts

Chapter 3
The Forerunner

◄·· ——————— ᴑ✦ᴑ ——————— ··►

I t was now early summer, in the month of Sivan on the Jewish calendar. Zechariah was an old priest who served in the Jewish Temple in Jerusalem. However, he lived in the outskirts of town in the province of Judea. Zechariah was born into the family of Abijah, the 8th division of the Levites. According to the ancient schedule for priestly service, the time had arrived for Zechariah to once again serve at the Holy Temple.

He set off on foot and headed for Jerusalem. He arrived at the Temple complex and found his living quarters for the week. Each morning, the assignments for the day would be announced. He visited with the other priests for a while before going to bed a little early. He was getting old, and the trip to Jerusalem was more tiring than usual.

The next morning, Zechariah awakened early. He recited the Shema prayer. "Hear O Israel: The Lord our G-d, the Lord is one. You shall love the Lord your G-d with all your heart and with all your soul and with all your might," (Deuteronomy 6:4–5). He donned his white, floor-length priestly robe and tied the sash around his waist. He placed the white turban upon his head and walked toward the place where the priests would receive their daily assignment. The Temple Mount always had a surreal atmosphere. Nevertheless, today there was a supernatural feeling that invaded the place like a fog. He tried to comprehend what was different, but it was like grasping at the wind.

Zechariah shook his head and brought his thoughts back to the morning tasks, which were about to be assigned. He gathered with the other priests in the Temple plaza. Quite unexpectedly, an announcement was made. His name was called out. *He* had been chosen to offer the incense in the Holy Place!

The altar of incense was in front of the thick curtain that separated the Holy Place from the Holy of Holies, where G-d lived. Within the fabric of the curtain, angels were embroidered in the design. Their sages taught angels *always* surround the presence of Adonai, in constant worship. In addition, since the time of King David, only descendants of Zadok, the High Priest during David's reign, could offer incense before the curtain.

This was a great honor, and he was humbled he had been chosen. Zechariah picked up the golden bowl of incense, which was made of frankincense and sweet spices. He slowly began to make his way to the Temple, where he would burn the fragrant incense. As he approached the Temple, he noticed a group of people praying outside the Temple courtyard. As he walked past them, they bowed slightly to him in reverence. They understood Zechariah would sprinkle the fragrant incense on the hot coals, on the golden altar of incense. Incense was a symbol of prayer. As their prayers were directed toward heaven, the incense would create smoke, likewise rising toward heaven, like a fragrant prayer.

Zechariah left the sunshine and stepped into the dimly lit Holy Place. He blinked a few times and waited for his eyes to adjust to the subtle light. He recognized each article of furniture, placed exactly the way every priest learned.

The altar of incense was straight ahead, in front of the tall curtain with the embroidered angels. He slowly walked down the center of the Holy Place, toward the golden altar, located at the end of the rectangular room. He glanced to his left and saw the beautiful golden menorah with the candles burning brightly.

Walking slowly, he tried to capture every detail, every smell, and every sight. He looked to his right and saw the golden table of show-bread. Earlier, freshly baked bread had been placed on the table, and it smelled delicious.

He continued walking until he finally reached the altar of incense. He stood directly in front of the ornate curtain. He reached his trembling hand out and gently touched the beautiful curtain. "This is a once-in-a-lifetime opportunity," he thought, "one I will never have again."

He remembered his task for the day. Moving closer, he sprinkled the incense onto the smoldering coals. Smoke quickly blossomed from the coals, floating toward the ceiling, like a gentle prayer.

As the smoke filled the room, Zechariah thought he saw movement near the altar. It startled him. He stepped back and squinted his eyes to get a better look. To his amazement, a huge angel stood to the right of the altar. Zechariah was terrified! He could feel his heart beating in his chest and his knees began to tremble. He thought he would collapse on the floor, but somehow, he was able to stand. The angel was twice as tall as a man. A holy fear fell on Zechariah as he pondered why the angel had appeared. He was frozen in place by terror.

The angel spoke and said, "Do not be afraid, Zechariah, for your prayer has been heard, and your wife Elizabeth will bear you a son, and you shall call his name John. He will be a joy and delight to you, and many will rejoice because of his birth, for he will be great in the sight of the Lord. He is never to take wine or other fermented drink, and he will be filled with the Holy Spirit even before he is born. He will bring back many of the people of Israel to the Lord their G-d. And he will go on before the Lord, in the spirit and power of Elijah, to turn the hearts of the fathers to their children and the disobedient to the wisdom of the righteous, to make ready a people prepared for the Lord."

Zechariah was shocked and could hardly speak, but he finally asked, "How can I be sure of this? I am an old man, and my wife is well along in years."

The angel sternly said, "I am Gabriel. I stand in the presence of G-d, and I have been sent to speak to you and to tell you this good news. And now you will be silent and not able to speak until the day this happens, because you did not believe my words, which will come true at their appointed time."

Zechariah was immediately speechless; he could not make a sound. He stared at Gabriel for a long time, thinking about his message. He and Elizabeth were going to have a baby? In their old age, this was a wonderful miracle. When they were younger, they had prayed to have a child. However, as they got older, they stopped praying *that* prayer, because it was impossible.

Now, Adonai had answered their prayer for a baby! The angel said his son would be used to *"make ready a people prepared for the Lord... in the spirit of Elijah."* This meant Adonai had also answered the prayers of generations of Jewish people, for their Messiah to come. Most students of the Tanakh knew the scripture where Malachi stated, "Behold, I will send you Elijah the prophet before the great and awesome day of the Lord comes."[4] (Malachi 4:5–6).

This announcement meant the Lord *Himself* would be coming to earth as their Messiah, as the Hebrew Scriptures had promised! Zechariah was frozen in time and space. Malachi was one of the last well-known prophets to speak about the coming Messiah. However, he spoke over 400 years ago. Therefore, some people had given up hope that Adonai would *ever* speak again or that the promised Messiah would come. In the past few years, some of the Zadok priests had prophesied the Messiah would be born soon. However, many of the Levitical priests were no longer religious, and they despised the Zadok priests. If a priest was a descendent of Zadok, he normally kept this a

---

[4] See prophecy 3 in the Prophecy Chart.

secret from the other priests. Nevertheless, Zechariah and his family *never gave up hope* that the Messiah would come. *They simply believed.*

Meanwhile, the people outside the Temple were waiting for Zechariah to come out, wondering why it was taking him so long. After Zechariah recovered from this shocking encounter, he made his way back outside. He wanted to tell everyone what he had seen and heard, but he could not speak. He began to move his arms and make signs, trying to show them an angel had spoken to him, but they could not understand him. Because of his inability to speak and the signs he made, they realized he had seen a vision while he was in the Temple (Luke 1:21–22).

When Zechariah's weekly service was completed, he traveled back home to be with his wife of many years, Elizabeth. Even though she had not been able to bear him a child, he still loved her passionately. His heart was full of excitement and joy. He could hardly wait to tell Elizabeth about his encounter with the angel and his good news. He had a spring in his step and was energized. He felt like a young man again. Of course, he would be forced to write it all down, in order to tell her, but he remembered *every* word the angel had told him, and he wanted to write it down anyway, so he would have a record of it.

After he arrived home, he told Elizabeth his amazing heaven-sent message by writing it down. As she read his words, big tears rolled down her checks. After decades of barrenness, they would finally have a baby to call their own. In addition, he would be used by the Most High G-d to announce the coming of the Messiah. She was completely overwhelmed by this news!

Elizabeth snuggled her head next to Zechariah's heart and gently cried while tears flowed down her face. The shame she had felt during the long, childless years flowed gently out of her body. These were tears of thankfulness for the kindness Adonai had shown them. Zechariah remembered the ancient prophecy, foretold by Isaiah, about a forerunner who would come *before* the Messiah[5] (Isaiah 40:3–5). *His* son would be this forerunner. He felt his eyes began to water, but he did not care; he let the tears flow freely.

Zechariah wrapped his arm around Elizabeth, wiped her tears away, and gently kissed her on the top of her head. Her hair was completely gray now, but he thought she would make a beautiful gray-headed mother. Deep in his soul, he *knew* the angel, Gabriel, had spoken a true prophecy.

Within a few weeks after Zechariah returned from Jerusalem, Elizabeth realized she was pregnant! This meant her baby would be born in the springtime, around Passover. It was such a wonderful and amazing miracle. She *knew* her son would be used by G-d. The women in town had mocked and ridiculed her for years. It was such a shame to not bear children for your husband. Therefore, she decided to stay hidden from them for several months. When she came out of hiding, it would be obvious to *everyone* she was pregnant. She told Zechariah, "The Lord has done this for me. In these days, he has shown me favor and has taken away my disgrace among the people."

Elizabeth was now on a journey of faith. She also knew her path was part of a larger plan; a plan which G-d had orchestrated. The angel had spoken, and she knew it would happen.

---

[5] See prophecy 4 in the Prophecy Chart.

Thought Provoking Journey:

- Zechariah was born into the family of Abijah, the 8th division of the Levites. This division was one of 24 similar, family lines which were descendants of the Jewish priestly line of Aaron, who was a descendent of Levi. Many centuries earlier, King David had arranged for each division to send representatives, twice a year, to Jerusalem to serve in the temple for one week. The other divisions worked in various support roles in the area surrounding Jerusalem. The priests would also work the weeks of the three, major Jewish feasts (Pesach, Shavuot and Sukkot), when all Jewish men were required to come to Jerusalem. This schedule provided for enough priests to work all of the 51 weeks of the annual Jewish calendar. The priestly schedule started over each year, in early spring with the month of Nisan, the first month on the Jewish religious calendar.

- In the Bible, in Ezekiel 44:15-16, the scriptures state that only the descendants of Zadok, the High Priest during King David's reign, were allowed to enter the Temple and minister before God.

- In scripture, there are different types of angels. Some angels are the messengers of God. They are sent to earth, to bring a message from God, to a man or a woman. Other angels are sent to earth to wage war as directed by God. A third type of angels are seraphim and they are angels of fire. They also surround God's throne and worship him continually.

- If needed, angels can take on the appearance of a man. But, if seen in their natural state, they are terrifying for humans to see.

- The story of Zechariah and Elizabeth is in the Bible, in Luke 1:5-25.

Chapter 3 Thoughts

Chapter 4
The Bridegroom Comes

In Bethlehem, the spring wheat harvest had been completed earlier, in time for Shavuot (Pentecost). It was now summer. The farmers would allow the shepherds to come into their fields, and the sheep would eat the leftover wheat stalks. The farmers had learned the sheep helped the ground to become more fertile for the following year. Each morning, the shepherds would meet and lead their sheep to fresh water and a new grassy area or newly harvested field for the day.

Josiah, Jonathan, and their father joined the group of shepherds waiting outside. Josiah began to look for his little lamb, born a few weeks earlier. As soon as they made eye contact, the lamb pranced over to Josiah and nuzzled his nose on Josiah's leg.

"I think I will give my lamb a name," Josiah said to his father.

"What name will you give him?"

Josiah thought for a minute and said, "I think I will call him Chamoodi because he is such a sweet and gently lamb." (Chamoodi, pronounced Ha Moody, means "my sweetie" in Hebrew.)

Samuel smiled, but Jonathan laughed and said, "That is what mothers call their little children, when they are being nice. But when they spill the water pitcher, they are called something different." They all laughed as they remembered the many times Josiah would spill the water that had been brought into the house. Josiah was very clumsy as a young boy.

Josiah simply turned to his lamb and said, "Bo, Chamoodi" (which means, "Come, my sweetie"), and the little lamb followed Josiah as the group led their flocks out of Bethlehem.

The shepherds were a close-knit group of men, and many of them were related. At nine years of age, Josiah was the youngest of all the shepherds in their group. He loved to spend time with these older men and listen to their stories. Moreover, he always asked questions.

As they walked, Josiah remembered he had an unusual dream during the night. In his dream, he could not see anything, but he could hear a young man singing a simple song. The words of the melody were "I know there's more than what teachers are teaching, I know there's so much more." The melody was sung two times with great earnestness, as if to impress upon the listener some critical piece of knowledge was known by the singer, knowledge that was elusive for most people.

In some mysterious way, the young man singing this melody had obtained a revelation. When Josiah woke up, he could hear the melody playing in his mind, over and over. The melody touched something deep within him. Josiah wondered, "What can be known if people are not teaching it?"

The song confused him but intrigued him at the same time. He made a mental note to ask his father in the morning when he woke up. Josiah slowly drifted off to sleep again, singing the little melody in his heart. It gave him comfort, almost as if his destiny was attached to this simple melody.

Now, he remembered the dream and wanted to share it with his family. "Father," Josiah said excitedly, as he hurried over to his father. "I had a dream last night, but I don't know what it means."

"Well, tell me your dream and I will try to interpret it for you," Samuel said jokingly.

"Okay, listen and I will tell you," Josiah said with enthusiasm and then shared his dream.

Jonathan looked intently at Josiah and asked, "You heard the same song two times? Did you know the number two represents the idea of a testimony or a witness? The Ten Commandments were written on two tablets, as a witness to humanity. Our law requires two witnesses for a testimony to be accepted by the council. This must mean your melody has been confirmed and your family should accept your dream. But what could it mean?"

Samuel quickly replied, "Josiah, do you remember the tower, where our new lambs are born? It is called Migdal Edar, which means the Tower of the Flock. The great Hebrew prophet Micah referred to *that* tower when he said, 'And you, O tower of the flock, hill of the daughter of Zion, to you shall it come, the former dominion shall come, kingship for the daughter of Jerusalem'[6] (Micah 4:8).

"Some of our rabbis privately say the area around *that* tower, the area where our sheep are born, will be the place where the birth of the Messiah will be announced. However, they do not teach it publicly yet. There are some prophecies in our holy scriptures that we do not fully understand yet; they have been *concealed*. But one day, the rabbis believe, the meaning of these mysterious writings will be revealed.

"There is a scripture in Daniel which states, 'There is a G-d in heaven who reveals mysteries' (Daniel 2:28). The rabbis believe G-d will give a revelation to our people about these prophecies. Maybe *that* is what your song means. Maybe it means the rabbis know *more* than what they are teaching; could that be it?"

Josiah shrugged his shoulders as if to say, "How would I know? I am only a nine-year-old boy."

"Josiah," Jonathan continued, "Did you know if you have the same dream three times, it means your dream is *truly* from G-d; did you know that? If you have that same dream two more times, make sure

---

[6] See prophecy 5 in the Prophecy Chart.

you tell us. I had a dream last week about a sheep caught in the bushes, down by the creek. I struggled all night with that sheep, trying to get him untangled from the bush. You were not there to help me. By the time I woke up, I was exhausted."

Josiah smiled, remembering the many times he had helped Jonathan, or his father, get a wayward sheep untangled and back to the flock safely.

"Come," Jonathan announced, "let's guide the sheep to another pasture so they can eat." Josiah followed his brother as they began to lead the sheep along an ancient path.

When they reached a pasture where the sheep could graze, the men sat down and soon began to eat the food that they brought. After they finished eating, it was time to lead the sheep to a small nearby brook.

Josiah called out, "Bo, Chamoodi!" (Come, my sweetie), and his little lamb came over and licked his face, removing all traces of the lunch he had finished. Josiah giggled and stood up to follow the rest of the shepherds. Chamoodi quickly followed, trusting his friend completely.

Josiah thought he was extremely lucky to work outside with his father and brother, taking care of the sheep. "What a great life," he thought. "This is the way of the shepherd."

As the summer days grew longer, Josiah helped the shepherds while Jonathan stayed home and worked on the addition to their father's house. He was making a place ready for his bride, Rachel. He worked long hours on this room and its furniture, and he hoped to have their wedding in the fall.

In the ancient tradition of the Jewish people, the father of the groom is the one who decides when the wedding will take place. The groom would send messages to the bride to let her know the time would be soon, but only the father of the groom knew the day and the hour when the groom would return to get his bride.

Therefore, Jonathan did not know when his father would make this important decision. He worked hard to get everything ready for the wedding and the marriage supper. From time to time, he would send his friend David with a message to Rachel, letting her know about his progress.

In Israel, for the Jewish people, their lives revolved around the weekly Sabbath, the seasons, and their religious feasts. There were seven feasts that G-d commanded the Jewish people to observe each year. The three feasts of Passover, Unleavened Bread, and First Fruits were back-to-back over a seven-day period of time and were sometimes simply called Passover. These three feasts occurred in the spring.

The next feast was Feast of Weeks (Pentecost), and it took place in late spring. The remaining three feasts (Feast of Trumpets, Day of Atonement, and Feast of Tabernacles) took place in the fall within a few weeks of each other. Three of these seven feasts required the men to travel to Jerusalem for the celebration. These three pilgrimage feasts were Pesach (Passover) in the spring, Shavuot (Feast of Weeks) in the late spring, and Sukkot (Feast of Tabernacles) in the fall.

Earlier in the year, Josiah and his family traveled to Jerusalem for Pentecost, when Jonathan's betrothal ceremony took place. Now, six months later, Jonathan and his father were planning to go back to Jerusalem for the Feast of Tabernacles. Jonathan hoped his father would give his approval for him to get Rachel for their wedding, while they were in Jerusalem. If Samuel approved, Jonathan would surprise Rachel. Then, she and her family would travel with them, back to Bethlehem for the wedding.

Now, in the hills surrounding Bethlehem, the weather was beginning to transition to fall. During this time of year, the shepherds traveled higher up the hillsides, and they would now spend the night with their flocks. It was too far to walk back to Bethlehem each night, and it was the mating season for the sheep. Therefore, the shepherds would carefully watch over their sheep during this time, especially at night.

Josiah loved it when he could sleep outside on a cool night, with the stars overhead and the other shepherds nearby. Josiah's little lamb, Chamoodi, born earlier in the spring, was his constant companion and usually slept next to Josiah.

When the sheep where grazing at these higher elevations, each morning a different person would leave the shepherd's campsite and walk back down the hillside to Bethlehem. Later, he would return with food and supplies for the group. Today, it was Samuel's turn to get supplies, so he took Josiah with him.

As they walked down the hillside, Josiah looked out over his world. He could see the little town of Bethlehem nestled in the valley below. Samuel began to speak in his teacher voice, "Josiah, in a few weeks, we will celebrate Sukkot, the Feast of Tabernacles. Jonathan and I will go to Jerusalem for a couple of days. Do you remember what we *do* during Sukkot?"

"Yes, father; I remember because *this* is my *favorite* feast," Josiah replied with gusto. "We will build a sukkah and have music and dancing and lots of food—for an entire week." As he spoke, he danced around with his arms held high, moving them as if he heard music.

Samuel laughed, nodded his head and replied, "Yes, this feast *is* the most joyful feast of them all. But there is more than food and music. Do you remember *why* we build a sukkah and *what* we are celebrating?"

"We build a sukkah to remind us that our ancestors lived in tents for forty years, after they left Egypt," Josiah replied in a matter-of-fact voice, reciting the age-old story.

"Good, you remembered," Samuel replied with approval. He continued, "The sukkah also reminds us G-d came down from heaven to live among us, in the tabernacle which Moses built. That is why *this* celebration is called the Feast of Tabernacles.

"But there is also *another* event which took place during this time. When King Solomon built the first Temple, it was dedicated during the Feast of Tabernacles. After he prayed the dedication prayer, fire came down from heaven and consumed the sacrifice, and the glory of the Lord filled the Temple. It must have been awesome to see. We will build our sukkah before Jonathan and I leave for Jerusalem, and you can help us."

As they continued down the hill, Samuel lovingly pulled Josiah closer and gave him a quick hug. They both smiled and continued to Bethlehem to gather supplies to take back to the waiting shepherds.

A few weeks later, every family in Bethlehem, and in fact *all* of Israel, was preparing for the Feast of Tabernacles. Near their home, each family built a temporary structure large enough for the family to eat their meals inside the structure. Some families would even sleep in their sukkah the entire week.

They assembled a roof of various branches and tree limbs, placed over support poles. They left space among the branches, which made up the roof, so they could see the night sky. They would sometimes hang white curtains on the sides of the structure to make the walls. This reminded them of the pillar of cloud that accompanied the first tabernacle, built by Moses in the wilderness. *That* tabernacle was also called the "tent of meeting" because G-d met with his people in that temporary tabernacle. The Hebrew word for "tabernacle" meant "dwelling place." Therefore, the tabernacle was *where G-d lived,* here on earth, and where he met with his chosen people, his beloved bride. Samuel and his entire family helped to build their sukkah. They were now ready for the Feast of Tabernacles.

The next morning, after everyone in the family was awake, Samuel called the family together. Samuel led the family in the morning Shema prayer and made an announcement. With a smile on his face, he announced, "Jonathan, I have watched the progress you have made on the addition to our house. So I have decided. Tomorrow, you and I will go to Jerusalem for the Feast of Tabernacles. On the next day, I give you permission to get your bride, Rachel!"

Everyone in the family exploded with shouts of joy. Josiah jumped up and down for a few seconds and ran over to his brother. Jonathan's smile was expansive as he nodded his head in agreement with his father. Rachel was coming to live with their family. Josiah's mother was crying and hugging Jonathan. Josiah's younger sister, Hannah, clapped her hands in excitement. Samuel and his wife had three children, and this was the first wedding for one of their children.

At sundown, the first day of the Feast of Tabernacles began. Samuel led the family in the evening Shema prayer before everyone went to bed for the night.

The next morning, after the Shema prayer, Samuel and Jonathan left for Jerusalem. Jonathan's faithful friend David also journeyed with them. Josiah traveled up the hills to help with the sheep for a couple of days. He had instructions to be back at home in two days to meet the wedding party as they returned from Jerusalem.

When Samuel, Jonathan, and David arrived in Jerusalem, they went to the same inn where they stayed for the betrothal ceremony, earlier in the year. David left to give Rachel a message: that her bridegroom would be coming soon and that she should get ready.

Once Rachel heard the message, she dressed in her best clothes, prepared her lamp, found her extra olive oil, and notified her bridesmaids to come stay at her house until her groom arrived. She did not know *when* Jonathan would come, so she had to be ready to leave at *any* moment, even if he came at night.

In the ancient marriage tradition, the groom would usually leave his house at night, with torches to light the way. He would arrive at the bride's house just before midnight, especially if they lived in the same city. Every groom hoped to find his bride ready and waiting, wide-awake with her lamps burning. Since Jonathan and Rachel did not live in the same town, Rachel wondered if her groom would come during the day instead of at night. If Jonathan came during the day, they would have time to walk to Bethlehem and arrive before dark.

It was the first day of Sukkot, and the streets of Jerusalem were crowded with Jewish men and women who were on pilgrimage in the holy city. Samuel and Jonathan made their way to the Holy Temple to offer their sacrifice. The Feast of Tabernacles (Sukkot) was the last of the seven annual feasts ordained by G-d. The Feast of Tabernacles was not only the seventh feast, but it takes place in the seventh month and lasts for seven days. This made the Feast of Tabernacles extremely important and symbolic because the number seven has a spiritual meaning. After G-d created the heavens and the earth in six days, G-d rested on the seventh day. Therefore, the number seven represents completion, fullness, and rest. Since the seventh day, also called the Sabbath, is considered holy, the number seven also represents spiritual perfection and holiness.

During this feast, several symbolic events took place on the Temple Mount in Jerusalem. One event was the Water Libation Ceremony, which was celebrated with great joy. Each day, the priest would walk to the Pool of Siloam, followed by large crowds. The priest would draw water from this pool with a golden pitcher. After the daily sacrifice, this water would be poured out on the altar with great ceremony. This water held prophetic meaning for the Jewish people. Years earlier, the waters of Siloam were used to anoint the kings of the House of David. Since the Messiah would come from the House of David, the water from the Pool of Siloam represented a future time when the Messiah would come. When the water was poured out on the altar, it also represented a promise made in Isaiah 44:3. In *that* Holy Scripture, G-d promised He would pour out His Spirit upon all flesh.

Samuel and Jonathan knew these scriptures. As they watched the water being poured out on the altar, they shouted with excitement and anticipation of their promised Messiah. The crowd also sang from Psalm 118. "Oh give thanks to the Lord, for He is good; for his steadfast love endures forever" (Psalm 118:1). Another favorite scripture from Psalm was sung with gusto: "The Lord is my strength and my song; he has become my salvation. Glad songs of salvation are in the tents of the righteous" (Psalm 118:14–15). In the Hebrew Scriptures, the word for "salvation" is the word "yeshuah." However, Yeshua had become a popular name for Jewish boys. It was spelled slightly different, but it also meant salvation and came from the same root word.

This scripture was sung every year during the Feast of Tabernacles, when the water ceremony took place. It reminded the Jewish people that yeshuah (salvation) would come to the tents (the tabernacles) of the righteous. It was a promise from Adonai that one day their Messiah would come. And they believed this promise! Some people believed the Feast of Tabernacles pointed to a future time when the Messiah would finally appear.

The singing at the Temple reminded Samuel he wanted to purchase a surprise gift for Josiah. He found a man who made musical instructions and bought a lyre for Josiah. Since songs were in the dreams that Josiah had, Samuel thought it would be good for his son to learn to play the lyre. Then, Josiah could play and sing the songs that he heard in his dreams.

Another event, which took place during the Feast of Tabernacles, was the nightly lighting of four giant menorahs in the Temple complex. Each menorah had four branches; at the top of each branch, there was a huge bowl that held 10 gallons of oil. These menorahs were 75 feet high, the height of a 7-story building. The Temple was built on a hill, so when these sixteen menorahs were lit, the entire city of Jerusalem was illuminated. The light from these menorahs could be seen for miles; it was a glorious sight. In fact, it was said when these menorahs were lit, a man could read a scroll at night on the Mount of Olives, over three miles away!

The Feast of Tabernacles reminded everyone of the pillar of cloud by day and the pillar of fire by night, when the children of Israel were in the wilderness. The cloud and the fire represented G-d's everlasting presence with His people. The light from the menorahs also reminded the people of how G-d's Shekinah glory once filled Solomon's temple, which was located in the very same spot as their renovated Temple now stood. This feast reminded everyone that G-d wanted to dwell in their midst.

Samuel, Jonathan, and David rejoiced with the crowds all day and most of the night before they finally made their way back to the inn to get some rest. It was the most exhilarating and joyful feast anyone could attend. Samuel led everyone in the evening Shema prayer before telling them it was time to go to bed.

Morning came and the men finally awakened. Samuel led them in the morning Shema prayer and said, "Jonathan, go get your bride. It is time to take Rachel to our house. We have a wedding to celebrate."

Jonathan smiled and nodded his head; he was ready. The three men packed their belongings and started toward Rachel's house; Jonathan was leading the way. As they approached Rachel's house, David blew his shofar to announce the return of the bridegroom. Rachel had been ready and waiting since David has shared his message the day before. Rachel flung open the door and appeared in a white, spotless gown. She was adorned with the gifts that Jonathan gave her at their betrothal. She was radiant! Jonathan and Rachel led the procession, and her bridesmaids and family joined the wedding group. They left Jerusalem and headed to Bethlehem.

Within a few hours, the wedding procession had walked to Bethlehem, where Jonathan's family and friends greeted them. The wedding took place under the sukkah, which was adorned with white fabric and beautiful flowers. Jonathan and Rachel spoke their vows to each other, in front of their parents and friends. Jonathan placed a small crown on Rachel's head and said she would be a queen to him forever. Jonathan told Rachel she would rule with him over their family. He placed a golden ring on her finger as a symbol of his everlasting love.

After the vows were spoken, a huge wedding feast took place under the sukkah. Every kind of food was displayed: roasted lamb, beef, and chicken. Jonathan's mother had baked delicate cakes with honey and nuts. There were various types of breads and soups. The best wine was served. The summer harvest had been plentiful, and they feasted on the bounty that had been collected a few weeks earlier. As part of the tradition for the Feast of Tabernacles, there was music and dancing late into the night. What a joyous celebration it was!

While everyone was singing and dancing, Samuel secretly left and came back with the lyre, his surprise gift for Josiah. When he came back, the lyre was hidden behind his back. He shouted, "Shalom, shalom!" to get the attention of the crowd.

"Josiah," Samuel began. "This is a special night for Jonathan, but I have a gift for you."

Josiah looked up at his father with a quizzical expression. "For me, father?"

"Yes, Josiah, I bought this in Jerusalem for you." He pulled the lyre out from behind his back and presented it to Josiah. The crowds clapped and shouted with their approval.

"How did you know I wanted a lyre," Josiah stammered.

"Adonai told me. And Adonai never lies," Samuel replied with a big smile as he handed the lyre to Josiah.

Josiah choked back his tears, looked up at his father, and said, "Thank you. I promise I will take very good care of it."

Josiah sat down and began to strum on the lyre and hum a little song. A neighbor who knew how to play the lyre sat down beside him and began to show him a few simple songs. Josiah's younger sister, Hannah, came over and tried to touch the strings of the lyre.

"No, Hannah, you are too little to play with this," Josiah said sweetly and gently moved her hands away.

"Hannah, come. Let's dance together." Samuel said playfully while he took her hands and began to distract her from the lyre. Hannah loved to dance, so she went with her father. Nevertheless, she kept looking at the new toy that her older brother now had.

It was a time to be thankful for many blessings. When the celebration was finished, Samuel led everyone in the evening Shema prayer, this time with Rachel repeating the ancient prayer along with her new family. Rachel and Jonathan moved into the room that Jonathan had completed earlier. During this time, by watching his father, Josiah learned what it meant to be a loving and patient father, a father who gives good gifts to his son. And life in Bethlehem was good for the shepherds and their way of life.

Rachael and Jonathan were beginning their marriage, blessed by Adonai. They were on the path to marital happiness, according to their ancient traditions.

Journey on the Ancient Path - The Way of the Shepherd
Chapter 4 - The Bridegroom Comes

Thought Provoking Journey:

- The Feast of Tabernacles reminded the Jewish people of God's presence in the wilderness, when God tabernacled, or lived, in the midst of His people after they left Egypt.

- King Solomon's Temple was dedicated during the Feast of Tabernacles and the Shekinah presence of God came down and dwelt in the Temple. God came to live in the midst of His people.

- The Feast of Tabernacles occurred in the fall, after the summer harvest had been completed. It was celebrated by enjoying the fruits of the harvest. It was the final feast of the year and the most joyous of all the feasts.

- At the end of time, God will live in the midst of His people, His bride, forever in heaven. Does this feast foreshadow a future, heavenly feast called the Marriage Supper of the Lamb?

www.ngcarraway.com

Chapter 4 Thoughts

Chapter 5
Angelic Visitation

At the end of the fall season, when Elizabeth was five months pregnant, she finally came out of hiding and shared the news of her pregnancy with her neighbors. They were all astonished and knew Adonai had performed a miracle for this righteous couple. Elizabeth had a relative named Mary, who lived in Nazareth, about a four-day journey north. Even though Mary was still a young woman, Elizabeth and Mary had a close relationship. Mary looked up to Elizabeth as a spiritual mother.

Mary was legally betrothed to a man named Joseph. However, in the Jewish tradition, Mary and Joseph lived separate lives during this betrothal period, just as Jonathan and Rachel had done.

Joseph was a descendent of King David and Abraham (Matthew 1:1–16). Mary herself was *also* a descendent of King David and therefore Abraham[7] (Luke 3:23–38). In the beginning of the holy Jewish scriptures, G-d promised all nations of the earth would be blessed through the Abrahamic lineage.[8]

---

[7] See prophecy 6 in the Prophecy Chart.

[8] See prophecy 7 in the Prophecy Chart.

Scholars of the Scriptures thought this blessing was referring to the promised Messiah. The Essenes prophesied that the Messiah would be born 70 generations after Enoch.[9] In addition, the prophet Micah stated that the Messiah would be born of the lineage of Judah. Both Mary and Joseph were descendants of Judah.[10]

When Elizabeth was six months pregnant, G-d sent the angel Gabriel to Mary with a message, *before* Mary and Joseph came together, as husband and wife. The angel Gabriel appeared to Mary and said, "Greetings, O favored one! The Lord is with you." The angel frightened Mary, and she was troubled by what he said. She wondered what his message meant.

Gabriel said to Mary, "Do not be afraid, Mary, for you have found favor with G-d. And behold, you will conceive in your womb and bear a son, and you shall call his name Yeshua[11]. He will be great and will be called the Son of the Most High. The Lord G-d will give him the throne of his father David, and he will reign over the house of Jacob forever, and of his kingdom there will be no end."[12]

Mary replied to Gabriel, "How will this be, since I am a virgin?"[13]

The angel answered, "The Holy Spirit will come upon you, and the power of the Most High will overshadow you; therefore the child to be born will be called holy; the Son of G-d.[14] And behold, your relative Elizabeth in her old age has also conceived a son, and this is the sixth

---

[9] See prophecy 8 in the Prophecy Chart.

[10] See prophecy 9 in the Prophecy Chart.

[11] When "Yeshua" was translated into English, it was incorrectly translated as "Jesus"; a better translation might have been Joshua. But his Hebrew name was Yeshua, which meant "salvation". Some scholars think the word also meant "God's salvation".

[12] See prophecy 10 in the Prophecy Chart.

[13] See prophecy 11 in the Prophecy Chart.

[14] See prophecy 12 in the Prophecy Chart.

month with her who was called barren. For nothing will be impossible with G-d."

Mary pondered on this for a minute; Elizabeth was pregnant? It was a miracle!

Mary said, "Behold, I am the servant of the Lord; let it be to me according to your word" (Luke 1:26–37).

The angel disappeared as quickly as he had appeared. Mary was stunned! She was going to have a baby? The angel said he would be called Yeshua, which meant "salvation." And her child would be the *Son of G-d!* This meant he would be *the Messiah* that all Israel had expected for centuries. She did not understand *how* this would happen, but she believed the angel.

All her life, Mary had heard the Messiah would come to Israel and deliver the Jewish people. The Hebrew Scriptures had prophesied the Messiah would be born of a woman. In the very beginning of creation, when Adam and Eve sinned in the Garden of Eden by listening to the serpent (who deceived Eve), G-d promised them the seed of the woman (a descendent of Eve) would be in a battle with the evil serpent. And eventually, someone *born of a woman* would bruise the head of the serpent.[15] But there was *another* prophecy, which stated the Messiah would be born of a young girl. Isaiah stated, "Therefore the Lord himself will give you a sign. Behold, the young girl (a virgin) shall conceive and bear a son, and shall call his name Immanuel"[16] (Isaiah 7:14).

The word "Immanuel" meant "G-d with us," and some people believed this scripture meant the Messiah would be born of a virgin because all young girls were virgins. This would be a supernatural conception and birth, an undeniable miracle! The Messiah, the Son of G-d, would live life on earth as a human being. If G-d came to earth in his

---

[15] See prophecy 1 in the Prophecy Chart.

[16] See prophecy 11 in the Prophecy Chart.

full glory, men would be frightened and reject any interaction with him, just as they did at Mount Sinai, over 1,300 hundred years earlier.

Mary recalled another prophecy about the Messiah, which Isaiah the prophet recorded years earlier. In Isaiah 9:6–7 it is written: "For to us a child is born, to us a son is given; and the government shall be upon his shoulder, and his name shall be called Wonderful Counselor, Mighty G-d, Everlasting Father, Prince of Peace. Of the increase of his government and of peace, there will be no end, on the throne of David and over his kingdom, to establish it and to uphold it with justice and with righteousness from this time forth and forevermore.[17] The zeal of the Lord of hosts will do this."

In the past, when Mary heard this teaching, she always wondered *who* would be the mother of this child. Now, the angel said *she* had been chosen to be the mother of the Lord. She decided she must travel to Elizabeth's house to share her exciting news. Since Elizabeth was already six months pregnant, this meant for three months, they would *both* be pregnant at the *same* time.

That night, she softly prayed the Shema prayer before going to bed. As she lay on her bed, she felt as if a heavy blanket had been placed over her entire body. She knew the Hebrew word "kavod" meant "glorious or the Glory of the Lord." But, "kavod" also meant something heavy or weighty. She felt like the Glory of the Lord had been placed on her body like a heavy blanket. She had a wonderful feeling of peace and total security. She did not understand *exactly* what has happening to her, but she believed G-d was at work *in* her. Mary thought to herself, "Sometimes, you must first believe, before you can understand."

She also thought about Joseph, the man she would soon marry. How would she explain to him she was pregnant but still a virgin? Would he believe her? She did not know how she would tell Joseph, but she felt completely at peace. As she drifted off to sleep, she simply trusted Adonai would work it out.

---

[17] See prophecy 10 in Prophecy Chart.

Soon after this supernatural visitation from the angel Gabriel, Mary traveled to the home of Elizabeth. It was now winter in Israel, which meant frequent rains. But Mary was thankful the temperature was not cold enough to freeze the puddles that covered the streets. When Mary arrived at the home of Zechariah and Elizabeth, she entered the home and greeted Elizabeth, who was 6 months pregnant. When Elizabeth heard Mary's greeting, the baby in her womb started to move. It felt like the baby was jumping. The Spirit of G-d fell on Elizabeth, and she loudly proclaimed, "Blessed are you among women, and blessed is the child you will bear. But why am I so favored, that the mother of my Lord should come to me? As soon as the sound of your greeting reached my ears, the baby in my womb leaped for joy. Blessed is she who has believed that the Lord would fulfill His promises to her."

Mary was shocked! How did Elizabeth know she was pregnant? She had told no one, not even Joseph. Mary felt a chill go down her back, and she shivered. It was a supernatural sign that the Spirit of G-d had spoken *through* Elizabeth to confirm what the angel had told Mary a few days earlier. Mary replied, "My soul glorifies the Lord, and my spirit rejoices in G-d my Savior, for he has been mindful of the humble state of his servant. From now on, all generations will call me blessed, for the Mighty One has done great things for me; holy is his name."

Mary stayed with Elizabeth for about three months. They had such sweet and tender conversations about what the future held—for both of them. The ancient prophecies foretold the Messiah would be the King of all Kings. The G-d of Abraham, Isaac, and Jacob had promised the Messiah would come and establish His everlasting kingdom in Israel. Mary and Elizabeth thought this meant the Messiah would force the wicked Romans to leave Israel, the homeland of the Jewish people. In addition, there would finally be peace in the land of Israel. Mary shared with Elizabeth that she was anxious to tell Joseph that she was pregnant. Mary was not sure what Joseph would say or do.

Elizabeth gently spoke, "God also chose Joseph to be your husband. G-d will reveal the truth to Joseph. Do not worry; it is in G-d's hand."

One night, Elizabeth remembered something her husband had shared years earlier. Zechariah told Elizabeth there was a tradition among some of the priests at the temple. When their linen clothes became old, they would tear the linen into strips and save some of the strips for the promised Messiah, to use as swaddling for when he was born. Every generation did this, expecting the Messiah to be born in *their* generation.

When it came time for Mary to return to Nazareth, Elizabeth gave Mary a basketful of linen swaddling clothes. Mary hugged Elizabeth and said her goodbyes. She took the basket and returned to her home in Nazareth. She was thankful the winter season was finished and Passover would soon come. She could now feel the baby moving inside her womb, and she knew Joseph must be informed.

Joseph was a carpenter and a stonemason. He was very talented and could build anything out of wood or stone. His workshop was also part of his house, as was the custom for most craftsmen in Nazareth. As Mary walked to Joseph's shop, she prayed for Adonai to give her the right words to explain how she became pregnant. But how does anyone explain an encounter with the Spirit of G-d? Especially if the other person has not had their *own* encounter?

Words are simply not adequate to convey the supernatural realm that exists and is more real than the natural world. Mary prayed Joseph would have his own encounter, so he could not deny what Adonai had done. It was late in the day when Mary arrived at Joseph's shop. She pushed open the door. Joseph looked up from his work, hammer in his hand, and smiled.

"You have returned from Elizabeth's house. I hope you had a nice visit. But I am glad you are back home, Mary."

"Yes, yes," Mary stammered, "I have something to tell you, Joseph... Elizabeth is pregnant in her old age. Her baby will be born very soon.

Her husband Zechariah had a visitation from an angel, who told him they would have a child. It's a miracle!"

"How amazing," Joseph replied. "We don't hear of miracles very often these days. But our Hebrew Scriptures tell of many miracles which have happened in the past."

"Joseph, I have something to tell you... about a miracle which has happened to me," Mary timidly began.

"You, Mary? You had a miracle? What happened, did you see an angel like Zechariah did?" Joseph quizzed.

"Yes, Joseph, before I left for Elizabeth's house," Mary slowly said, "an angel appeared to me."

"The angel said I was favored by G-d. The angel told me I would conceive and give birth to a son, even though I am a virgin. The angel said this child would be holy and He would be called the Son of G-d. He is the Messiah!" Her voice was shaking as she spoke, and her brown eyes were pleading for Joseph to understand.

Joseph interrupted, "What do you mean? Mary, you are pregnant?"

"I, I... don't understand," he blurted out. "You talk about an angel, but no, this can't be true. You speak foolishness. You have not been faithful to me, as you pledged."

"No, Joseph! It was the Spirit of G-d that came upon me, I promise; I have not been with a man. I fear G-d and I honor you too much to do such a thing! There is a child inside of me; I can feel him moving already. He will be born in about six months. Miracles do happen! You must believe me," Mary implored.

"Please leave, Mary, I can't think right now. I thought we, I mean I though you... no, you need to go now," Joseph snapped.

"Joseph!" Mary pleaded with tears running down her face. "Please let me explain. The Spirit of G-d came—"

"No!" Joseph grunted as he threw his hammer to a nearby table. He turned his back to Mary. "Go home, Mary. I have work to finish."

A single tear began to slide down Joseph's face. He hurriedly wiped it away as Mary turned and left. Her sobs were ringing in his ears as he shook his head.

"How could she do this?" Joseph pondered. "She is such a sweet and kind young woman, but this is shameful! She is a righteous person, or I *thought* she was. I planned a future for us. But this! It is unacceptable. I must divorce her, according to the law. Nevertheless, I will do this in private and quietly. I don't want her to be scorned and ridiculed by our neighbors."

Joseph was frustrated. He could not keep his mind on his work. It was late in the day, anyway. He hurriedly ate his dinner and went to bed, thinking about his plan to divorce Mary. Joseph said the Shema prayer before he went to sleep. But that night Joseph did not sleep well. He had a most unusual dream. In his dream, an angel appeared: "Joseph, son of David, do not fear to take Mary as your wife," the angel said. "For that which is conceived in her is from the Holy Spirit. She will bear a son, and you are to give him the name Yeshua, because He will save His people from their sins" (Mathew 1:18–21).

Joseph awakened, stunned! His encounter with an angel, even in a dream, convinced him Mary was telling the truth about the baby she carried.

This child was conceived by the Holy Spirit of G-d! It was so hard to believe, even though the Jews had prayed for years for their Messiah to be born. And Mary was still a virgin! She had not betrayed him after all. He felt terrible about the way he had treated Mary.

When morning came, he quickly dressed, said the Shema prayer, and went to Mary's house. Mary was sitting in a corner, her shoulders were slumped over, and her eyes were red and puffy.

"Mary," Joseph said tenderly. Mary stood up and searched Joseph's face for some indication of why he was there. "Mary, I had a dream last night. An angel spoke to me. I believe you. I have come to take you home with me."

Mary collapsed in his arms with sobs of relief. Her prayers had been answered. G-d provided Joseph to serve as the baby's *legal* father, even though Joseph was not the biological father of the baby she carried.

Mary stared intently into Joseph's eye. "G-d chose *me* to carry this child. But, *you* were also chosen by G-d."

Mary knew Joseph would protect her and the baby she carried and provide a safe home for them. Mary and Joseph got married and Mary went with Joseph to his house and legally became his wife. However, they slept in separate areas of the house and did not consummate the marriage until after Yeshua was born. Mary knew she was on a journey ordained by G-d himself.

All this took place to fulfill what the Lord had said through the prophet Isaiah: "Behold, the virgin shall conceive and bear a son, and shall call his name Immanuel"[18] (Isaiah 7:14). Pesach (Passover) would be coming soon. Joseph and Mary would celebrate it as a family, according to the ancient traditions.

---

[18] See prophecy 11 in Prophecy Chart.

Thought Provoking Journey:

- The Bible does not tell us anything about Mary's mother or father. And, the Bible does not specifically state how Elizabeth and Mary are related. Because of their age difference, many scholars believe that Mary's mother, and Elizabeth, were sisters. But, we will never really know unless some ancient manuscript is discovered which explains their relationship.

- God can do the impossible and the miraculous; He will fulfill His word according to His plan and in His time.

- Is it possible that Mary became pregnant during the Feast of Hannakuh, the Feast of Lights?

- In Hebrew, Mary's real name is Miriam.

- The Hebrew word for 'God with us' is spelled Immanuel or Emmanuel, depending on the translation.

- The story of the angel's visit to Mary, and the birth of Yeshua (Jesus), is in the Bible in Luke 1:26-38, Luke 2:1-21 and Matthew Chapters 1 and 2.

- The story of Elizabeth and Mary is in the Bible in Luke 1:39-56.

- In Luke 3:23-38, the genealogy of Yeshua (Jesus) is listed through Mary's lineage. Mary was apparently the daughter of Heli. Mary's husband, Joseph, was the son of Jacob, as explained in Matthew 1:16. Luke shows that Yeshua was born 70 generations after Enoch. And, according to Luke, Yeshua was born 77 generations from Adam. The number seven represents perfection and the completion of God's work. God rested on the seventh day after creation, because his work was finished and it was perfect. The number ten represents God's order. There are ten commandments and God required a tenth of the increase as a tithe from the Israelites. This means the numbers 70 and 77 have spiritual meanings. The timing of Yeshua's birth meant God's work, to provide a Messiah, was perfectly in order and was perfectly complete.

Chapter 5 Thoughts

Chapter 6
First Sacrifice

It had been several months since Josiah received the lyre from his father. He would often play simple songs for the shepherds while they watched their sheep. The men thought Josiah was talented when he played their traditional Jewish songs.

Passover would be coming soon, and Josiah would go up to the Holy Temple for the first time. He was thrilled. Ever since Josiah went to Jerusalem last year, for Jonathan's betrothal, he found himself thinking about Jerusalem. It was such a beautiful city with grand buildings, fountains, pools, and gardens. Jerusalem was so different from the little town of Bethlehem with its dusty roads and rocky hills.

Josiah and the other shepherds were staying at the Tower of the Flock again for a few days, waiting for the new Passover lambs to be born. When night came, Samuel led everyone in the Shema prayer and Josiah played the lyre while the men sang a few songs. Each person found a place to sleep. Since Josiah was the youngest, he was allowed to sleep in the tower on the small bed. Josiah hung his lyre on the wall of the tower. As usual, Josiah allowed Chamoodi to sleep next to him. Chamoodi gazed into Josiah's eyes with complete trust. Josiah returned the affection with a quick hug. Chamoodi had such soft wool. Josiah drifted off to sleep, his little lamb snuggled up next to his chest.

That night, Josiah had a dream. He dreamed he was inside a small, dark cave. However, the sun was shining outside, so the opening to the cave resembled a white circle of light. In the dream, Josiah had laid down in the cool cave to rest. He had just closed his eyes when he heard someone coming into the cave. He sat up and looked at the cave entrance. There was someone blocking the light; the front of the person could not be seen, it was in a shadow. The light from outside the cave made a halo effect around the person. The person spoke; it was breathy, almost like a soft wind blowing. The person said, "Resurrection and life." Then, Josiah woke up.

He was not frightened, but he could feel a cool wind blowing around him, and he wondered whether there was an angel nearby. What did this dream mean? And why was he having so many dreams lately? He made a mental note to tell his father about this dream in the morning.

The next morning, after the Shema prayer, he shared his dream with the other shepherds while eating breakfast. When he mentioned the word "resurrection," the men began a lively discussion about the concept of resurrection. Most of the Jewish people, including the Pharisees, believed in the resurrection of the physical body after death. However, the Sadducees, who were the ruling elites, did not believe in the resurrection.

As the group of shepherds discussed Josiah's dream, their contempt for the Sadducees was evident. The shepherds were amazed that someone as young as Josiah would have a dream about such a grown-up topic. But no one had any idea what such a dream could mean. To have a resurrection, you must first have a death. Was it a warning of some kind?

This year, Josiah would help take the sheep to the Temple complex to be sold for the Passover sacrifices. Josiah was now ten years old. He would be allowed to actually watch the sacrifices take place. He was not sure he was ready for that. His little sheep, Chamoodi, would be one of the lambs sacrificed for Passover. Chamoodi was dear to him, and he could not stand the thought of losing him. He sighed to himself and thought, "I guess this is part of growing up."

One night, after the family had completed their evening meal at home, Samuel asked Josiah to play some music. Josiah eagerly reached up and took down his lyre. He sat down on the floor and began to play a familiar song. The entire family joined in and sang several songs together. Jonathan and Rachel sat side by side. His little sister, Hannah, danced and twirled in the midst of everyone.

After dancing to a few songs, Hannah came over and reached for Josiah's lyre. "No!" shouted Josiah as he pushed Hannah with one hand and lifted his lyre with the other hand.

Samuel jumped up and spoke harshly to Josiah. "Josiah, don't push your sister." Hannah, angry at being pushed, immediately rushed toward Josiah.

"Hannah, leave him alone," their mother said as she tried to grab Hannah.

It happened in an instant. Hannah reached for the lyre. Josiah tried to stand up to get the lyre out of Hannah's reach. However, as he stood, he tripped and fell. The lyre fell to the floor and one of the wire strings broke in half. Hannah dove for the lyre. Miscalculating her effort, her face hit the wire. Hannah screamed as blood began to pour out of her face. The wire had pierced her cheek, leaving a gash.

By now, all of the adults were on their feet trying to separate the kids and move the lyre. Josiah's mom tried to soothe Hannah by holding her tight and rocking her back and forth. Rachel brought a cloth and placed it on Hannah's face, trying to stop the bleeding. Josiah was rubbing his leg where he fell and hit the ground. Samuel was holding the broken lyre with an astonished look on his face. He had never seen his children act this way. Now, his lovely daughter was crying and bleeding from her face.

Jonathan gently took the lyre away from Samuel and said to Josiah, "Come, let's go outside for a few minutes." Josiah was crying as he followed his brother.

"I didn't mean for Hannah to get hurt," he stammered, the tears flowing freely.

"I know. It was an accident. Hannah should not have jumped on you. It's not your fault."

"She is always trying to get my lyre, but she is too little. Will she be okay? She was bleeding a lot." Josiah sighed. "But it *was* my fault, I pushed her first." Josiah was wiping his eyes as Samuel came outside.

"Josiah," Samuel said sternly, "I know you did not intend to hurt Hannah, but you should never push your sister."

"I, I, I'm s..s..sorry, father," Josiah stammered, looking at the ground. He could not look his father in the eyes.

"Come inside now," Samuel replied sternly, as they all walked back inside the house.

Hannah was still sitting on her mother's lap, with a blood-stained cloth held to her cheek. Her robe was also covered in blood. Josiah could see his mother had been crying.

"Hannah, I am sorry. I did not mean to hurt you," Josiah mumbled to Hannah. He had never seen that much blood. He felt his stomach twist inside of him, and he felt weak. He quickly moved to the corner of the room and sat down. He stared at the floor without moving.

He could hear his mother sobbing quietly and Hannah's whimpers. For a long time, no one moved, no one said anything. Everyone sat in stunned silence. After a few minutes, Samuel slowly and deliberately began to recite an ancient blessing over Hannah.

Slowly, Hannah stopped crying and looked at her father, blinking her eyes. Everyone felt a tangible shift in the atmosphere of the room. Hannah smiled slightly and took the cloth down from her face. The bleeding had stopped. Rachel gently wiped her cheek with a wet cloth until all the blood was gone. The gash in her cheek appeared to have closed. She would probably have a scar but not a big one. Josiah's mother hugged Hannah tightly as she wiped tears from her eyes.

Samuel spoke to his family. "I think we are all tired and ready for bed." He prayed the Shema prayer and gently kissed Hannah on the top of her head, as her mother carried her to bed. Samuel hugged Josiah and gently directed him toward his bed.

Josiah lay on his bed, thinking. He realized the magnitude of what *could* have happened that night. "I should never have pushed her away," he kept thinking. "I should have been patient and kind like my parents. I am a failure!" His mind created various what-if stories. When Hannah fell on the lyre, *what if* the wire had pierced her eye instead of her cheek, she would now be blind in that eye! That would be terrible, and it would be his fault. What if she had broken her arm; that would be terrible as well. She might never be able to use her arm to take care of herself or a family. He had a realization that his actions could result in lifelong tragedy for others. He scolded himself and decided he would try to *do* better, to *be* better.

A few weeks later, Josiah traveled with Samuel, Jonathan, and the other shepherds from Bethlehem to Jerusalem, a few days before Passover. The shepherds took over 1,500 sheep to Jerusalem to be sold and used for the Passover sacrifices. It was a constant job to watch over that many sheep and make sure none of them strayed off the ancient path. Eventually, they made it to Jerusalem, entered through the Gate of the Essenes, and took the sheep to the holding pens near the Temple Mount. Only Chamoodi was allowed to stay with Josiah. Since they had a free day before the actual Passover ceremonies began, Josiah and his father had time to explore the city. They stayed in the Essene Quarters again, at the same inn, close to Rachel's family.

The following morning, after the Shema prayer, Samuel took Josiah around the city. He showed Josiah the various merchants who were selling pottery, fabrics, and olive oil, among other items. As they walked, Samuel showed him some of the famous buildings in the city and explained the history of Jerusalem and their people. However, he saved the trip to the Temple Mount for Passover.

"Josiah, you have learned from our Holy Scriptures that G-d made the entire world and everything in the world, and it was perfect," Samuel explained. "At first, G-d created the heavens and the earth, the sun, the moon, and the stars. Then, he created the trees and vegetation. Next, G-d created the birds, the fish in the oceans, and all the animals on the earth. G-d called his creation the Garden of Eden, and it was good and perfect. G-d then created the first man, whom he named Adam. G-d created Adam from the dust of the earth. Later, G-d created Eve, but not from the dust. Eve was created from a rib taken out of Adam."

"Yes, I have heard the creation story many times. It's amazing to think Adonai created all of the animals and the first man and woman."

"Well, there is one thing you may not have heard, because it is not written in our scriptures. But our sages tell us when G-d created the Garden of Eden; it was created here in Jerusalem."

"Really? No, I did not know."

"Yes! G-d used clay from the Garden of Eden to create humanity. It all started here, in Jerusalem. That is one reason why Jerusalem is the most holy and important city in the entire world. Years later, G-d showed Abraham the place where he wanted Abraham to offer his son, Isaac, as a sacrifice to Adonai. Of course, that was simply a test to see if Abraham would obey G-d's request. Abraham did *not* need to sacrifice his son because Adonai supplied a ram to use instead."

"I have heard that story many times," Josiah replied with excitement.

"I am sure you have, my son," Samuel nodded his head. "But did you know the very location where Adonai showed Abraham for *that* sacrifice is located on the Temple Mount?"

"What? No, I did not know. No wonder Jerusalem is such a holy place."

"Yes. Our Holy Temple sits on the *very* spot where Abraham was willing to sacrifice his son Isaac. G-d had a plan for the location of His Temple long before Jerusalem was a city. G-d will often hide a mystery from everyone, and years later reveal what the mystery means. But remember, Adonai our G-d never lies!"

"Incredible!" Josiah gasped. "It's hard to image this was the Garden of Eden. Now, this area is a dry and dusty place. It does not look like a garden at all. At least Herod built pools and fountains."

"You are correct. Jerusalem does not look like a garden now because of man's sin," Samuel explained. "When Adam and Eve sinned against G-d, the entire world suffered because of their sin. Now, hard work is needed to produce food, to provide a place to live and clothes for our family. However, in the beginning, it was not this way. The Garden of Eden was a place of provision, security, and fellowship with Adonai. There was nothing to fear in the Garden."

"Josiah, have you heard the story of how G-d provided the first clothes for Adam and Eve, after they sinned?"

"No, I don't think so."

"After Adam and Eve sinned, they realized they needed clothes, and they tried to make clothes by sewing fig leaves together. Of course, that did not work. So Adonai *Himself* killed the first animal and G-d made clothes for Adam and Eve from the animal skins.

"Our Holy Scriptures tell us that life is in the blood. The reason we are required to offer a sacrifice is to make atonement for our sins. The blood makes atonement for the soul. So G-d shed the blood of an animal, an *innocent* animal, in order to atone for the sin which Adam and Eve committed against G-d."

Josiah was listening intently. He had deep furrows in his forehead as he tried to process this information. He thought, "An innocent animal must die, so humans can be forgiven? So *that* is what the sacrifice means!"

"Josiah, Chamoodi can stay with you tonight. But tomorrow at sundown, Passover begins," Samuel said softly. "Do you know what this means?"

"Yes," Josiah spoke softly with his face downcast. "Tomorrow, Chamoodi, my sweet lamb, must be sacrificed."

"Yes, tomorrow afternoon, we go up to the Temple Mount." Samuel gently hugged Josiah.

Later than night, Josiah lay down in the bed, with Chamoodi next to him. He placed his arms around Chamoodi and softly said, "I love you, my little lamb." Chamoodi fell asleep in the embrace of his loving shepherd. In Josiah's mind, he could see his beautiful Chamoodi in the green pastures of Bethlehem. Josiah felt a tear run down his face, which he quickly brushed away.

White lamb

When morning came, Josiah quickly dressed and met with the other shepherds for breakfast. Samuel led everyone in the Shema prayer, and they ate the food provided by the inn. However, Josiah did not have much appetite. He was excited about going up to the Temple for the first time, but he was anxious about the sacrifice. This afternoon, their family in Bethlehem would join them in Jerusalem for the Passover meal.

Samuel and Josiah left with the other shepherds and headed for the holding pens near the Temple Mount. For several hours, the shepherds worked to sell the lambs they had brought to Jerusalem. It was now early afternoon on Nisan 14, and Passover would officially begin at sundown. Their sacrifice would be made near 3 in the afternoon, and the lamb would be roasted for the Passover dinner that night.

As Josiah followed his father and Jonathan up the steps leading to the Temple complex, the beauty of the various buildings, arches, and courtyards stunned him. Chamoodi followed Josiah everywhere he went, never leaving his side. Once they reached the massive courtyard of the Temple, Josiah saw the glorious Temple for the first time. He was overwhelmed by its golden brilliance. He knew he was standing in a sacred place.

The outer courtyard was crowded with groups of families. Each family had a lamb to be sacrificed. Only men were permitted into the Court of the Israelites, the inner courtyard where the sacrificial altar stood. Samuel and Josiah entered. As they waited their turn, Josiah looked around at the splendor and majesty of this holy place. He saw the bronze altar that contained a fire. Several priests were lined up in a row, each one holding a cup with a round bottom. The line of priests extended to the bronze altar. Other priests were in the background reciting a passage from Psalm and playing musical instruments. The sights, the sounds, and the smell overwhelmed his senses. The priests were arranged in such a way that several lambs could be slaughtered at the same time, to speed the process for the thousands of families who were present.

When their turn came, Samuel held Chamoodi in his arms, almost like a baby. Josiah gently stroked Chamoodi's head. As the lamb looked into the eyes of his trusted shepherd, it seemed as if the little lamb smiled. Big tears welled up in Josiah's eyes as he said, "I will never forget you, Chamoodi."

Samuel knelt down and held Chamoodi on the ground in such a way that the lamb could not move. Jonathan helped to hold the lamb tightly, making sure that he could not kick and perhaps break a leg. It was important that none of his bones were broken in the process of the sacrifice. Another priest knelt close by with an empty cup. As Josiah watched, the priest took his sharp knife and quickly cut the lamb's throat. Chamoodi stared at Josiah in shock, as if to question why this had happened. He made a final gurgling sound as the blood began to flow from his throat. Josiah wept.

Death for Chamoodi came quickly; it was done with the utmost care to prevent unnecessary pain or torture. The priest then said, "It is finished." The priest collected the blood in the cup. When the cup was full, another cup was ready. The first cup was handed to the line of priests, who passed the cup until it reached the last priest, standing close to the bronze altar. The last priest poured the blood on the altar, making the sacrifice complete.

The first priest continued to work on Chamoodi until the lamb was skinned, cleaned, and ready to return to Samuel. As Josiah watched, tears streaming down his face, his father explained, "Without the shedding of blood, there can be no forgiveness of sin."

Josiah thought about the times when he had been angry or disobedient to his parents. He remembered the times he had been mean to his little sister. He certainly remembered the time he pushed her, and she gashed her check. He never wanted to do those things. He was immediately remorseful after such actions and decided he would try to do better, to be a kind person and more considerate.

He thought to himself, "Did Chamoodi die because of *my* sins, *my* mistakes?"

In his mind, he remembered the story of Adam and Eve and the first animal that was killed by Adonai, in order to cover their bodies and their sin. Josiah had a revelation. Adonai performed the first animal sacrifice in the Garden of Eden. What if that *first* animal sacrifice had taken place where he was standing, on the Temple Mount... where years later, other animals would be sacrificed? Was that possible?

To Josiah, it was fitting that Adonai would pick this place for the first sacrifice. Josiah also knew the Temple Mount was the location where Adonai told Abraham to take Isaac. Then, Adonai provided a ram for the sacrifice. Adonai picked the Temple Mount as the location for *that* sacrifice, so maybe he picked the Temple Mount as the location for the *first* sacrifice in the Garden?

Josiah continued to ponder about the importance of the Temple Mount in Jerusalem. He tried to understand why *this* spot of land was so special to G-d. Their sages taught the Garden of Eden was actually located in Jerusalem, and G-d used the dirt of the Temple Mount to create Adam. Was it possible that G-d loved this location *so much* because His plan was to have fellowship with man, *at this very location,* ever since the creation of the world? After Adam and Eve sinned, G-d still wanted to have fellowship with humanity. So was it possible He planned to have His Temple built on the same spot? Humanity could then come and fellowship with him at this very special spot. Sometimes Josiah felt the presence of G-d, but most of the time, G-d seemed very far away.

Many of their scriptures did not make sense to Josiah. They were a mystery when they were read in the synagogue. Were they written to point to a future event? Maybe some scriptures were symbolic and pointed to the *real* thing to come later, similar to a prophecy. Was that possible? If so, they could not be understood until the future, real thing happened. Something concealed now would be revealed later. There were so many mysteries in their scriptures; it would take a lifetime to understand them all. So, he pondered, what was the mystery of the sacrifice and the temple? What was the real meaning?

His father tapped his shoulder and said, "Come, Josiah, we must prepare for the Passover meal tonight."

As Samuel carried the lamb that had been slain, he gently placed his arm around Josiah.

Josiah walked with his head down; he could not bear to look at the dead lamb that his father now carried. When they reached the inn, his mother and sister had arrived, along with Rachel. The women began to prepare food for the Passover meal while Samuel and Jonathan started a fire and roasted the lamb. It would be the main course for dinner tonight.

Josiah felt like he was in-between worlds. His beloved Chamoodi had been sacrificed and would be served as the meal tonight. He had never felt this way before. It felt as if someone had punched him in the stomach. It was at least an hour before he could stop crying. He had no appetite for anything, especially for lamb. He could not bring himself to eat any lamb tonight, maybe never!

Everyone else was happy; it was Passover. Josiah's mother and father were busy preparing the food. Even though it was a solemn time, they were also cheerful and would sometimes start singing an ancient hymn.

Jonathan and Rachel had now been married for about six months. Jonathan had only been gone for a couple of days, but Rachel was overjoyed to see him. She kept whispering in his ear. He would smile and nod his head.

The entire family celebrated the traditional Passover Seder meal. Samuel led the family through the various parts of the meal. Their hands were washed, the blessing was spoken, the bitter herbs eaten, and the story of the Exodus shared while the meal was consumed. At the conclusion of the meal, they sang a few songs. Jonathan read a passage from the Song of Solomon. The last sentence in the passage was "I am my beloveds, and my beloved is mine," which Jonathan quoted softly while staring at Rachel.

"Rachel and I have an announcement to make," Jonathan finally shared. "Tonight, I found out she is pregnant. We are going to have a baby, and I am going to be a father!"

"Adonai has heard our prayers!" shouted Samuel. Josiah's mother was crying happy tears, but she still kissed Rachel on both cheeks. Everyone hugged Jonathan and Rachel. Josiah even managed to smile for the first time today.

"We think the baby will be born in six or seven months, maybe right after the Feast of Tabernacles," Jonathan explained.

"We will pray for a boy who will grow up to be a shepherd like us," Samuel interjected.

"Yes, a boy who will help us with the sheep, like Josiah is doing," Jonathan continued. "He will learn the way of the shepherds."

Everyone continued to rejoice with Jonathan and Rachel until it was time to go to bed. Samuel led the family in the Shema prayer, and each person retired to their bed for the night. Josiah felt lonely. Normally, Chamoodi would be sleeping next to him. He could still see Chamoodi's dark eyes staring at him, questioning why Josiah allowed his death. Josiah had traveled the path to the Temple for the first time and offered his first sacrifice, as instructed by the ancient law. He knew this was the way of the shepherd, but he still cried himself to sleep.

Thought Provoking Journey:

- Jerusalem and the Temple Mount have always been important to God. He picked out this location himself, for the events which would happen later.

- The Temple Mount is also the location God showed to Abraham for the sacrifice of Isaac, (which God did not require). Abraham did not pick the location, God did.

- King Solomon's Temple, and King Herod's Temple, were built on the same spot where Abraham offered a sacrifice, as directed by God.

- Did God perform the first animal sacrifice, to clothe Adam and Eve, on the Temple Mount to foreshadow the future Temple sacrifices?

- Most Christians know that Passover, and the sacrifice of the perfect lamb, foreshadowed the crucifixion of Jesus at Passover. Jesus was the Lamb of God, slain from the foundation of the world, crucified for the sins of humanity. (Revelation 13:8)

- Passover is the first of seven feasts ordained by God. (Leviticus 23) When God ordained these annual feasts, his master prophetic timetable and clock was set in motion.

- Each feast had a natural explanation, as well as a prophetic implication. These feasts foreshadowed future events; these feasts were 'pointers' on God's timeline. Sometimes, there were multiple, future events represented by a single feast.

Chapter 6 Thoughts

Chapter 7
The Spirit of Elijah

Zechariah had watched in amazement, as Elizabeth's stomach area grew larger and larger during the winter. He was still in shock over this miraculous pregnancy and the fact he would soon be a father. He was not able to speak at all. If he wanted to share a message, he was forced to write it down. Somehow, Elizabeth understood what he was thinking by looking at his face. They wept many happy tears as they felt the baby kicking inside her body.

Mary left their home a few days before they expected the baby to arrive so she would be home in time for Passover. For over 500 years, there was a Passover tradition practiced by Jewish families. On the Sabbath *before* Passover, Malachi 4:5–6 was read in all of the Jewish synagogues. This passage of scripture reads: "Behold, I will send you Elijah the prophet before the great and awesome day of the Lord comes. And he will turn the hearts of the fathers to their children and the hearts of children to their fathers." Jewish sages explained that the "day of the Lord" was the day when the Messiah would come. So this scripture revealed that Elijah would come *before* the Messiah arrived. In preparation for the coming of Elijah, when the Passover table was set, a place was reserved for Elijah.[19]

The time came for Elizabeth to give birth, and it was Passover. She gave birth to a son, as the angel had prophesied to Zechariah, 9 months earlier. All of their neighbors came by and rejoiced with this elderly couple, who now had a new baby son. It was the Jewish tradition to name a baby when he was circumcised. When the time came to circumcise the baby, all of the neighbors said he must be named Zechariah, after his father. Quickly, Elizabeth said, "No! He is to be called John!"

Her neighbors were amazed and admonished her, "There is no one among your relatives who has that name." Thinking Elizabeth was out of order, they said, "Let's ask Zechariah what he would like to name the child."

Zechariah asked for a writing tablet and to everyone's astonishment, he wrote, "His name is John."

The neighbors were stunned! In the past, the Zadok priests, the righteous priests who had been displaced from the Temple over a hundred years earlier, some of them were called John. But they wondered why Zechariah would choose this name.

As soon as Zechariah wrote this declaration, his mouth was opened, and his tongue was set free; he could speak! Zechariah began praising G-d and sharing about his angelic encounter, 9 months earlier. Zechariah explained the angel of the Lord said this baby would "go on before the Lord, in the spirit and power of Elijah, to turn the hearts of the fathers to their children and the disobedient to the wisdom of the righteous, to make ready a people prepared for the Lord."

Everyone was amazed as they remembered the scriptures about Elijah that were read just before Passover. They were seeing a prophecy fulfilled in their lifetime. The prophecy about Elijah, which had been

---

[19] See prophecy 3 in Prophecy Chart.

concealed in Malachi, was now revealed to the people in Judea. It seems G-d would often hid, or conceal, a prophecy in the holy Jewish scriptures. Later, when the prophecy came to pass, G-d would then reveal what the prophecy meant. But until the prophecy was revealed, there was uncertainty about the prophecy, because it was concealed and the meaning was hidden.

Then, Zechariah was filled with the Holy Spirit and he began to prophesy, "Blessed be the Lord G-d of Israel, for he has visited and redeemed his people... And you, child, will be called the prophet of the Most High; for you will go before the Lord to prepare his ways, to give knowledge of salvation to his people in the forgiveness of their sins, because of the tender mercy of our G-d, whereby the sunrise shall visit us from on high to give light to those who sit in darkness and in the shadow of death, to guide our feet into the way of peace" (Luke 1:68–79).

The neighbors were perplexed. The Essenes were sometimes called the Sons of Light. Now, Zechariah was talking about light coming to people in darkness. And Zechariah prophesied his son, John, would be a prophet of G-d. The Zadok priests were the only ones declaring prophecies these days. Surely, these were amazing and wonderful times, and their Messiah would finally come. All of the neighbors were awestruck, and news of this miraculous event spread throughout the hill country of Judea. The people said this child was born with the spirit of Elijah, during Passover. Everyone was talking about this child and what he would do when he became a grown man. It was evident the Lord's hand was on him, even before he was born. Zechariah knew his son would walk the path of a prophet, as men of old had done hundreds of years earlier.

News of this miraculous birth quickly spread among the priests who worked at the Temple in Jerusalem. Since Zechariah was one of these priests, everyone knew him, and they knew he and his wife were too old to have a baby. Some of their ancient writings prophesied that the Messiah would be born seventy generations after Enoch. Many rabbis calculated that enough time had passed for the seventy generations to have occurred. They wondered how soon the ancient prophecies about their Messiah would be fulfilled. God was surely at work in their midst and this gave them hope.

Journey on the Ancient Path - The Way of the Shepherd
Chapter 7 - The Spirit of Elijah

Thought Provoking Journey:

- If John the Baptist (as he was called as an adult) was born during Passover, this would be a partial fulfillment, of an ancient prophecy, about a forerunner before the Messiah appeared.

- A second, complete fulfillment will happen at the end of time, just before the Messiah's second return, when another 'Elijah' will appear.

- If John was born during Passover, this would mean Mary's baby would be born in the fall, because John was six months older than Yeshua (Jesus).

- Today, the Jewish people still reserve a place for Elijah, at their Passover table.

- The Zadok priestly lineage had several men with the name of John. Did this name have a hidden meaning for this baby which was born to Elizabeth? Is it possible that John the Baptist was born of the Zadok priestly lineage?

www.ngcarraway.com

Chapter 7 Thoughts

Chapter 8
Days of Awe

When Josiah and his family took their sheep to Jerusalem for Passover, they heard the news of the Temple priest and the miraculous birth of his son. Everyone marveled that an angel had appeared and spoken a prophetic word and that G-d had performed a miracle. The local rabbis began to teach this child was coming in the spirit of Elijah, which meant the Messiah could come at any time. It was exciting times! Life for a shepherd in Bethlehem revolved around the weekly Sabbath, the Jewish religious feasts, and the seasonal changes. Passover had now come and gone.

Josiah was now considered "one of the men" and he enjoyed learning about the places where they could find grass during each season. He was taught to take the sheep from one field to the next, starting in the spring on the lower side of the hills. As the weather got warmer and the grass began to sprout at higher elevations, they took the sheep higher up the hillside. The shepherds would constantly move to places that had green pastures and water.

Josiah loved being up in the hills. He could look down below and see Bethlehem and the main road that meandered through the town. If you wanted to travel to Jerusalem and the cities beyond, you would travel north on that road. If you left Bethlehem and traveled south, the road would take you to Hebron, Beersheba, and even to Egypt. Soldiers, merchants, shepherds, and townspeople traveled this road.

Josiah would watch the changing parade of people as they came in and out of Bethlehem. Most travelers simply came into Bethlehem, stopped for water, and continued on their journey. However, there were a couple of small inns in the city for those who wanted to settle down for the night.

Samuel had been teaching Josiah about the Jewish calendars. He explained the Jewish people had two calendars. One calendar was considered the civil calendar, that began when G-d created the heavens and the earth. The second calendar was the religious calendar, and was introduced by G-d himself at Mt. Sinai. The religious feasts were determined by the religious calendar, which begins in the spring.

In the fall, there were three feasts celebrated by the Jews. All three feasts took place during the month of Tishri. The first feast was called Rosh HaShana, which meant "head of the year" (it was also known as the Feast of Trumpets) and was celebrated on Tishri 1. This was also the New Year on the civil calendar. The second feast was called Yom Kippur (the Day of Atonement) and was celebrated on Tishri 10. This was the most holy feast of all. The third feast was called Sukkot (Feast of Tabernacles) and was celebrated for a week from Tishri 15 to Tishri 21. Last year, Jonathan and Rachel were married during the Feast of Tabernacles. One day, before the month of Tishri arrived, Samuel explained to Josiah the importance of this month.

"Josiah, did you know Tishri is the most important of all the months on our calendar?" Samuel inquired.

"No, why is this month so special?"

"Well, Tishri is the seventh month, and two of our holiest feast days occur in this month; the Feast of Trumpets and the Day of Atonement. I have been teaching you how to determine when a new month begins; do you remember?"

"Yes, I remember," Josiah affirmed. "Our calendar is based on the moon. The first day of the month is when two witnesses have seen a new moon. And there is always a *full* moon on the fifteenth of the month."

"You are correct," Samuel nodded his head. "Let me tell you about Rosh HaShana, also called the Feast of Trumpets. When we hear a trumpet blown, we remember the time G-d came down on Mount Sinai with the sound of trumpets, thunder and lightning, smoke and fire.

"So this feast is a time to remember the giving of G-d's holy Law. This feast is the beginning of a ten-day period we call the Ten Days of Awe. This ten-day period will end on the Day of Atonement. On Rosh HaShana, G-d opens a book about your life. Inside your book are the deeds that you have done during the past year. On Rosh HaShana, G-d will judge you for those deeds."

Josiah's eyes opened wide and he moved closer to his father. Samuel continued, "G-d has three books with the names of all people. These books are called the Book of the Righteous, the Book of the Wicked, and the Book of the In-Between. On Rosh HaShana, G-d judges your behavior from the past year, and he will write your name in one of these books. Obviously, you want G-d to write your name in the Book of the Righteous."

"Yes, I want my name to be written in *that* book!" Josiah exclaimed.

"Our people blow trumpets on this day to tell people to 'wake up, repent, and get ready for judgment.' During the Ten Days of Awe, if you think G-d has written your name in one of the *other* two books, you should humble yourself and repent, hoping G-d will change his mind.

"On the Day of Atonement, G-d will make his final decision. During this time, G-d also decides who will live or die the following year. It is a very serious time, a time for you to contemplate your actions over the past year.

"Did you know that on the Day of Atonement, there is a special ceremony at our Holy Temple in Jerusalem? You already know only the priests are allowed inside the Holy Temple, and only the High Priest is allowed into the Holy of Holies," Samuel said with great reverence.

"And the High Priest is only allowed to enter the most holy place once a year. That day is on the Day of Atonement. Something very special takes place on that day. I plan to take you to Jerusalem this year for Yom Kippur so you can see for yourself what happens on this most holy day."

Josiah looked intently at his father and wondered what could take place at the Holy Temple on the Day of Atonement, but he dared not ask.

When the Feast of Trumpets finally arrived, all of the townspeople heard the blare of trumpets coming from the local synagogue. Each person bowed their head in prayer and began to think about the judgment that would come in ten days. It was a very sober day, and several people decided to fast and pray all day.

Josiah spent the next few days strumming his lyre while thinking about his actions over the past year. Sometimes he would sing a simple song of repentance. When he remembered being unkind to his parents or being short-tempered with his sister, he would ask Adonai for forgiveness and mercy.

Finally, it was time to travel to Jerusalem for the Day of Atonement. Jonathan was not able to go because Rachel was pregnant, and he did not want to leave her. So Samuel and Josiah went with a few other men from Bethlehem.

As they walked the ancient path to Jerusalem, Samuel began to speak, teaching Josiah about the meaning behind the Day of Atonement (Yom Kippur).

"Josiah, I am sure you remember how the Ark of the Covenant was placed inside the Temple which Solomon built. The golden ark was placed in the Holy of Holies, the small, room at the back of the Temple. No one was allowed to enter this room except the High Priest.

And the High Priest was only allowed to enter once a year to perform a very special act.

"Over a thousand years ago, G-d gave instructions to Aaron, the first High Priest, to perform a national act of repentance on this day. An animal would be sacrificed on the bronze altar and some of its blood put in a bowl. The High Priest would take this bowl and enter the tabernacle, walking toward the curtain which separated the Holy Place from the Holy of Holies, where G-d lived.

"The High Priest first had to repent for any personal sins. Then the High Priest would ask G-d to forgive all of the people for their sins from the previous year. The curtain, which separated the two areas of the Temple, was woven in such a way that it was four inches thick. In addition, the curtain was attached to the ceiling and to the walls on each side. Some people believe the High Priest traveled *supernaturally* through the fabric of the curtain.

"Somehow, the High Priest would enter the Holy of Holies and sprinkle some of the sacrificial blood on the top of the golden Ark of the Covenant. If the High Priest had not followed G-d's specific instructions or had not truly repented, he would be struck down, killed by G-d's holy presence. But if G-d accepted the sacrifice, the sins of the past year, for all the people would be forgiven."

Josiah gasped when he heard G-d's holy presence could actually kill the High Priest if he had not truly repented.

"Since *only* the High Priest could enter the Holy of Holies, it became a practice for the High Priest to wear a rope around his ankle in case he died while he was in the Holy of Holies. If he died, other priests would be able to pull him out by the rope. The High Priest also wore bells on the bottom of his clothing. While he was alive and moving, the sound of the bells could be heard outside in the Holy Place. But if the sound of the bells stopped, this meant he had died."

"Look, we are almost at the Gate of Jerusalem," Josiah shouted with excitement.

Old Jerusalem Gate

"Yes. You enjoy coming to Jerusalem now. Tomorrow, we will go to the Holy Temple for Yom Kippur. You will be amazed at what happens."

As they entered through the gate and walked down the streets of Jerusalem, Josiah was struck by the holy atmosphere that was evident inside the city. Everyone was solemn and reclusive, as if in prayer. It was very different from the last time he was in Jerusalem, at Passover. They reached the inn where they would stay overnight and went to bed early. Tomorrow, the Day of Atonement would be a busy day and they would walk back to Bethlehem before dark.

The next morning, after breakfast and the Shema prayer, Josiah and Samuel began to walk. They first went to a local synagogue where a special service was already underway. The men were solemn and repentant in their prayers. After the service, they walked toward the Holy Temple, high up on the Temple Mount. Josiah noticed all of the shops (at least those owned by Jews) were closed, in observance of this most holy day.

As they walked, Samuel began to speak again, in a holy tone of voice. "Today, you will experience something you have never experienced before, Josiah. You will see the power of the Living G-d, Adonai. And you will hear the High Priest pronounce the holy name of G-d."

"What? I thought G-d's real name could not be spoken."

"Our Holy Scriptures teach us that G-d's name *is* holy, and we dare not speak it. We use the word 'Adonai,' which means 'Lord,' instead of speaking the actual name. But, on this day, the High Priest is able to utter the name of our G-d when he speaks a blessing over us.

"You know in the scriptures there are four Hebrew letters which spell G-d's name; those letters are YHVH (yod- hey- vav- hey), but those letters are only consonants. Our written Hebrew alphabet does not have any vowels. Of course, there are vowels spoken in speech, but only the consonants are written. This makes it difficult to know how to pronounce G-d's name, by reading only the letters in our scriptures."

"You already know there are different types of sacrifices. Not all sacrifices are animals, we also have grain offerings. When a grain offering is made, oil and frankincense are poured on top of it. When the priest burns the grain, the frankincense will make a pleasant aroma to the Lord.

"But today, the priest will sacrifice a bull and other animals for Yom Kippur. The High Priest will take the blood of the animal, and he will enter the Holy Temple. The first area inside the Temple is called the Holy Place. This is where the priest burns the holy incense, a mixture that contains frankincense along with myrrh, cinnamon, spices, and olive oil. The holy incense is placed on the fire which is burning on the altar of incense, in front of the curtain."

Samuel gently pushed his way through the crowd, bringing Josiah with him, until they were near the door of the Temple.

"Today, the High Priest will walk through the Holy Place and enter the Holy of Holies, on the *other* side of the curtain. Years ago, the golden Ark of the Covenant was placed inside the Holy of Holies. In those days, the High Priest would sprinkle the sacrificial blood on the top of the golden Ark. However, the Ark disappeared years ago. So now, when the High Priest enters the Holy of Holies, he sprinkles the blood on the foundation stone which once supported the Ark.

"When the High Priest sprinkles the blood on the stone in the Holy of Holies, G-d will decide if the blood has been accepted. If accepted, the sins of our people will be forgiven for the past year. Look; do you see the High Priest coming?"

Josiah stood on his toes and moved around until he caught a glimpse of the High Priest near the Brazen Altar, where the sacrifice would take place.

"Yes, I see him," Josiah whispered. "He is barefoot and wearing all white."

Samuel spoke softly and said, "They are now sacrificing the bull and putting some of its blood in a bowl. Now, watch the High Priest."

As they watched, the High Priest walked to the door of the Holy Temple. Another priest followed with the bowl of blood. The High Priest took a rope that had been dyed a bright crimson color, and he nailed it high on the door of the Temple, so everyone could see. The rope was about an inch wide and several feet long.

The High Priest turned to face the men in the Court of the Israelites. With great ceremony, he took the bowl of blood from the priest, held it up high for all to see. He opened the door of the Temple and slowly walked in. The huge door with the scarlet rope slowly closed behind him.

"Watch the rope carefully," Samuel instructed Josiah in a whisper. The crowd became quiet; no one moved or made a sound. All eyes were on the scarlet rope nailed to the wooden door. It was as if time stood still. Josiah was not sure what would happen next or how long it would take. But he kept his eyes on the scarlet rope.

After what seemed like an eternity (but was probably only a few minutes), he could hardly believe what he saw. The rope slowly began to lose its bright scarlet color and turned a bright white! He gasped as did hundreds of other men watching this supernatural event. The crowd let out a collective sign; the white color of the rope meant Adonai had accepted the blood and the sacrifice. G-d had forgiven their sins for the past year!

The men began to whisper among themselves, nodding and smiling and pointing to the rope. While they waited, Samuel explained to Josiah: "Israel is the holiest land in the entire world and Jerusalem is the holiest city in Israel. The Holy Temple is the holiest site in Jerusalem. Inside this Temple, the Holy of Holies is the holiest location in the entire world. The holiest people in Israel are the priests, and the High Priest is the holiest of them all.

"Today, the Day of Atonement, is the holiest day on the calendar," Samuel continued in a whisper. "The Hebrew language is the most holy language, and the name of YHVH, when spoken in Hebrew, is the most holy word ever spoken. Once a year, on this day, the High Priest enters the Holy of Holies, in the Holy Temple in Jerusalem to sprinkle the sacrificial blood. It is a supernatural, spiritual occasion when the G-d of heaven decides whether to accept the sacrifice."

"We are truly blessed because G-d has forgiven our sins. And Adonai, our G-d, never lies! Now, watch what happens next."

The large door to the Temple slowly opened, and the High Priest stepped out into the sunshine. He stood on the top step where everyone could see him.

The High Priest slowly lifted both arms, outstretched at shoulder height. His palms were facing the men with his fingers making the holy sign of the priestly blessing. The shape of his hands formed a pattern of open spaces. Tradition taught that the openings in the priest's hands were to allow the glory of G-d to pass through to the people, as the blessing was spoken.

As Josiah watched intently, the High Priest began to recite the ancient High Priestly Blessing: "YHVH bless you and keep you. YHVH make His face to shine upon you and be gracious to you. YHVH lift up his countenance upon you and give you peace" (Numbers 6:25–26).

Each time the name of YHVH was spoken, it seemed to supernaturally leave the mouth of the High Priest by itself. The Shekinah glory of G-d was speaking through the mouth of the High Priest! Each time the name of YHVH was spoken, the people felt an invisible force hit them like a wave.

Josiah felt his legs buckle and found himself kneeling on the stone platform. All the strength left his body, and he could barely hold up his head and chest. He noticed his father and all of the other men in the courtyard were affected the same way. As far as he could see, men were on their knees with their heads bowed low.

The men replied, "Baruch shem kavod, malchuto le olam va'ed," which means, "Blessed be His name, whose glorious kingdom is forever and ever!"

Josiah was amazed at what he just heard. When the rabbi in Bethlehem said this blessing, he used the word "Adonai," but the High Priest spoke the holy name of G-d! The High Priest slowly walked through the crowd of men and left the Temple area. Josiah was still trembling on the inside. It was an experience he would never forget.

After a few minutes, Samuel slowly rose to his feet and helped Josiah up. "Josiah, I have been to Yom Kippur many times since I was your age, and I am always humbled and amazed by the presence of G-d when the blessing is spoken. May you never forget our G-d is holy, powerful, and just."

They walked through the courtyard and headed to the stairs that would lead down to the city of Jerusalem, below the Temple Mount. As they walked side-by-side, holding on to each other for support, Samuel continued, "This is the ancient path which our forefathers have walked for centuries coming to and leaving the Temple Mount. If you can understand G-d's prophecies about the coming Messiah and the importance of the feasts which He has commanded us to observe, you will learn the heart of G-d."

Josiah silently made a promise to Adonai to study and learn as much as he could from their Holy Scriptures. Each Sabbath, he was taught by their local rabbi about the commandments of G-d and the prophecies about the coming Messiah. Nevertheless, when he had a supernatural experience like today, he also learned something about G-d that books cannot teach. The experience brought a deeper understanding of the scriptures.

The next feast, the Feast of Tabernacles, would be in a few days. They would be home in Bethlehem to celebrate with their family and friends. It was the way of the shepherd.

Thought Provoking Journey:

- During the time of Yeshua (Jesus), the name of God (YHVH in Hebrew) was holy and only spoken by the High Priest and only spoken on special occasions.

- Today, the true pronunciation of YHVH is unknown. Some people think it may be Yahweh, Yehovah, Yahavah or Yiwah; but no one knows for sure.

- The famous High Priestly Blessing can be found in the Bible in Numbers 6:24-26. This blessing was once spoken only by the High Priest. Now, this blessing is spoken by many people, over their family.

- The Feast of Trumpets is also known as Rosh HaShana. Is it possible this feast, with the blowing of the trumpets, foreshadows the coming rapture of the church, when trumpets are blown? The earlier four feasts (in the spring and summer) foreshadowed events which have already occurred. These events occurred in the exact order of the spring and summer feasts. If this pattern continues, the Feast of Trumpets is the next prophetic feast to be fulfilled.

- Yom Kippur, which follows the Feast of Trumpets, is known as the Day of Atonement; a day of judgement for past sins. Is it possible this feast foreshadows the coming judgement day in heaven, known as the Great White Throne Judgement?

- Jewish tradition states that God created Adam and placed him in the Garden of Eden. They believe the location of this garden was Jerusalem. They also believe God took dirt from the Temple Mount to create Adam.

- Currently, on the Temple Mount, a building called the Dome of the Rock stands were the ancient Jewish Temple once stood. The Foundation Stone, where the Ark of the Covenant once stood, is in the center of this building.

- Jewish tradition states the Foundation Stone is where God told Abraham to take Isaac for the sacrifice.

Chapter 8 Thoughts

Chapter 9

Salvation at the Tower

Mary was now almost 9 months pregnant. The Feast of Tabernacles (Sukkot) would begin in a few days. This meant Joseph was required to be in Jerusalem for at least one day of the seven-day feast. Because of her large belly, Mary could hardly walk. She knew her baby would be born soon.

To make matters worse, Caesar Augustus, the emperor of the entire Roman Empire, had recently announced a census would be taken of every person in the Empire so he could tax them. Each family was required to return to the town of their ancestors and register with the Roman authorities. Joseph's ancestors were originally from the town of Bethlehem.

Even though Mary was pregnant, she was now required to travel with Joseph to Bethlehem, about 80 or 90 miles away, for the census. Thankfully, Joseph had a donkey upon which she could ride, instead of walking. As she prepared for the journey, she began to pack all the necessary items for her and the baby.

As a virgin, she obviously had never given birth, so she was not completely sure what to expect. However, she had cousins and aunts who had given birth, and she loved to hold their newborn babies. She carefully folded the strips of linen that Elizabeth had given her. These strips, made from the discarded priestly linen robes, would be used to swaddle her newborn baby. She also took extra strips of cloth to bath the baby after he was born and a change of clothes for herself.

Over the past few months since they married, Joseph had been a wonderful husband to Mary. He was gentle and thoughtful, and he slept in a different room. He would often ask if she needed anything. He was a devout man and very knowledgeable about the Hebrew Scriptures, especially the prophecies concerning the Messiah. They would often discuss the message that the angel told him in the dream: "That which is conceived in her is from the Holy Spirit. She will bear a son, and you shall call his name Yeshua, for He will save His people from their sins."

Yeshua was a very common name for boys in Israel at the time. Several boys in Nazareth had already been given this name. Mary and Joseph wondered what the angel meant by "He will save His people from their sins." They thought surely the angel meant the baby, which Mary carried, would save his people from the oppressive Roman rulers as well.

The following morning, Mary and Joseph loaded up the donkey, and they headed to Bethlehem. Mary rode the donkey while Joseph tried to lead the donkey on the smoothest path possible. Joseph expected the trip to take about four or five days. They first traveled south along the Jordan River, where the land was flat and there was plenty of water. At night, after they had traveled as far as Mary could go, they would stop at an inn to rest and replenish their food supplies. After a few days, they left the Jordan River and traveled west to Jerusalem, their last stop before reaching Bethlehem.

Joseph decided to spend the night in Jerusalem because there was an abundance of inns. Tomorrow night at sundown, the Feast of Tabernacles, Sukkot, would begin. It was truly the most joyful of all the feasts that the Jews celebrated. Joseph had been to Jerusalem for this feast many times in his life. However, Mary had never attended Sukkot in Jerusalem.

During the night, Mary began having birth pains in her abdomen, and she knew her baby would come soon. She could only hope Joseph would find them a comfortable place to stay in Bethlehem before the baby came. The following morning, Joseph and Mary started on the journey to Bethlehem. It was only about five miles from Jerusalem, so the trip would take maybe three hours, depending on how Mary did. As they traveled, every few miles, Mary would double over from the pain.

In an effort to take her mind off the pain, Joseph began to tell her about his previous trips to Jerusalem for Sukkot. "The week of Sukkot is absolutely the most joyous time in all of Israel," Joseph shared. "There are musicians at the Temple compound, and people are singing, dancing, and rejoicing with excitement. It is like the entire country is having a huge celebration.

"Did you know each day of this weeklong feast the High Priest will walk to the Pool of Siloam and draw a golden pitcher of water? The source of this water is the Spring of Gihon. Years ago, King Hezekiah built a tunnel that directed a continuous flow of water from the Spring of Gihon to the Pool of Siloam. Because the water flows constantly, it is called 'living water.' It was not stagnant like the water in some pools. This water will be poured out on the Altar, in the Temple courtyard, with great ceremony, every day during this feast. Thousands of people watch and rejoice with the High Priest."

Joseph glanced at Mary and noticed she was listening intently, as she held on to the donkey with one hand and her belly with the other hand. He continued, "Our tradition tells us when Solomon, the son of David, was anointed king many years ago, the water from this spring was part of the anointing ceremony.

"The prophet Isaiah said, 'With joy you will draw water from the wells of salvation.' So the Pool of Siloam is now known as the Well of Salvation," Joseph proclaimed.

"I did not know that," Mary said softly, deep in thought. "How interesting!"

"Isaiah also said Adonai will pour water on the thirsty land and make streams on the dry ground," Joseph continued. "Then, G-d said 'I will pour my Spirit upon your offspring, and my blessing on your descendants' (Isaiah 44:3). Our rabbis teach this water is symbolic of a day when the Spirit of G-d will be poured out on all flesh. They teach this will happen during the days of the Messiah, the anointed descendant of King David. And salvation will come to Israel!

"For centuries, during this feast, the water ceremony has been symbolic of a time when the Spirit of G-d will be poured out on the people, during the future Messianic age. That is why there is such rejoicing during the water ceremony.

"Those attending the water ceremony also sing verses out of the book of Psalm. In Psalm 118:14–15, it states 'The Lord is my strength and my song, he has become my yeshuah (salvation). Glad songs of yeshuah (salvation) are in the tents (tabernacles) of the righteous.

"Mary, that verse, about yeshuah has been sung during the Feast of Tabernacles for centuries," Joseph said with awe. "Now, your child, Yeshua, may be born during this important feast. This is incredible; only G-d could plan such an event!"

Mary smiled and nodded her head. She knew everything about this birth was related to a master plan that G-d had set in motion. She believed G-d was directing every part, from the conception of this special child to the future life which lay ahead for him. With the next labor pain she felt, she relied on her faith that G-d would help her during the birth of *His* son, the baby whom she carried inside her body.

They had traveled for several hours while Joseph shared his knowledge of this Feast. "Look, Mary, we must be getting close to Bethlehem. I see a building." However, as they got closer to the structure, Joseph's face dropped.

"I'm sorry, Mary," he said in dismay. "It's an abandoned building, some type of stone tower. But there is a little stream behind the tower. Why don't you get off the donkey for a little rest, and I will let him get a drink of water." Joseph did not know the stone tower was the first building located in the area called Bethlehem, which was less than a half mile ahead.

Mary slid off the donkey, holding her belly. She stifled her cry as she bent over in agony. The pain was intensifying with every hour. As soon as the donkey had drunk his fill, Mary got back on the donkey, and they headed down the road. They quickly reached the main part of Bethlehem and were shocked to see so many people. They thought everyone would be headed to Jerusalem for the Feast of Tabernacles.

As they navigated through the crowds, Joseph realized the throngs of people were in Bethlehem for the Roman census. In front of each home, a sukkah had been built for celebrating the Feast of Tabernacles (Sukkot).

Joseph knew there were a couple of inns in Bethlehem, and he directed his donkey to the first one, only to learn it was full. Mary groaned and silently implored Joseph with her big, brown eyes. The pain she felt in her body was evident on her face. She felt like she might give birth at any minute.

Joseph hurried to the other inn only to discover it was also full to capacity. Joseph begged the innkeeper to find a place for them since Mary was pregnant and could give birth any hour. The innkeeper did not budge; his place was full. But he shared with Joseph that there was an empty stone building, on the road to Jerusalem, which they could use. He explained the building was a watchtower used in the spring by the local shepherds. The shepherds would stay in the tower during the birthing season for their sheep. It was very primitive, but at least they would have shelter and privacy, and a nearby stream of fresh water.

Joseph remembered the stone tower. They had stopped there for water on their way into Bethlehem. It was getting late in the afternoon, and the sun would soon set. It was the best he could do under the circumstances. He asked the innkeeper if there was a midwife who could be sent to the tower tonight, to help with the birth. The innkeeper had a relative who was a midwife, and he agreed to send her to the tower.

Reluctantly, Joseph turned around. By the time they reached the stone tower, Mary was completely doubled over in labor pains. Joseph pushed open the wooden door to the building and found a small bed, lanterns on the wall, a couple of chairs, and a small table. There was a water pitcher and a basin on the table, along with cloth rags. In the corner of the room, there was a small fireplace where a fire could be built, either for warmth or for cooking. There was also a stone feeding trough inside the tower. Joseph thought it was a little odd that a feeding trough for animals would be inside the tower. Then, he remembered this tower was used during Passover when new lambs were born. The feeding trough even had some hay in it, left over from the last time it was used. Two small windows could be opened for fresh air.

Joseph went back to where Mary was waiting and gently helped her dismount from the donkey.

"Mary, there is a small bed in this building. You can lay down and get some rest while we wait for the midwife."

"Oh, Joseph, thank you so much. This trip has been exhausting," Mary said softly. Joseph led Mary into the building and helped her to the bed.

"Mary, there is a stream out back. I will get some fresh water and build a fire. Then, I will light the lanterns; it will be dark soon."

Joseph went to the stream for water. He was not sure what midwives did when a baby was born, but he knew they needed water in order to bath the baby. He started a small fire; the fall weather meant the nights would be chilly. It was not the inn where he hoped to stay, but there was no room at the inn. At least they were in Bethlehem, the hometown of his ancestors. He would register for the census in the coming days and then decide what to do.

As the sun began to set and the stars began to shine, Joseph mused about the timing of this baby. The Feast of Tabernacles had arrived and would last for a week. The tabernacle represented a time when the children of Israel wandered in the desert for 40 years, before they came into the Promised Land. Moses built a portable tabernacle, and the presence of G-d rested in the tabernacle. Therefore, the first Tabernacle was a place where G-d came to live among his people. Now, the Son of G-d would be born during the Feast of Tabernacles. A sign G-d had come down to earth, once again, to live among his people. Joseph considered for over a thousand years, since the first Tabernacle was built, this feast held a hidden meaning. Would the true meaning of this feast be revealed with the birth of this baby?

Joseph heard a knock on the door. The midwife had arrived. She said her name was Ruth. Joseph introduced her to Mary, who was now in full labor.

"Mary, everything will be okay," Ruth said with assurance. "I have delivered many babies in Bethlehem. Is this your first baby?"

"Yes, this is my first pregnancy. In fact, I am still a vir... , I mean yes, and this is my first baby."

"Joseph, I see you have built a fire and lit the lanterns. Will you bring one to me so I can see?" Ruth implored. "And bring me a basin of water. Do you want to stand at Mary's feet and watch your baby when he is born?"

"Oh, no! I do not want to watch," Joseph gasped. "In fact, I am not the baby's fath... I meant to say, I am, never mind, no, I will stand over here in the corner and let you deliver the baby."

Ruth moved Mary so the lantern provided the light that she needed. Ruth asked Mary a few questions about how long she had been having contractions. She could tell Mary was trying to push. The baby was about to come out.

"Mary, your baby will be born soon. When you feel the need to push, do it. I will use these clothes to catch your baby when he comes out."

As Ruth watched for the baby's head to appear, she looked again and said to herself, "What is happening? I don't understand this..." She looked again and thought to herself, "This young girl is a virgin! Am I seeing things?"

Ruth tilted her head and looked at both Mary and Joseph, wanting to ask questions, but she did not have time. Mary let out a slight scream, and the baby's head came out, followed by his entire body.

"Mary, it's a boy," Ruth explained. "Let me cut the cord and clean him up; then you can see him."

"Yes, we knew it would be a boy," Mary said softly. "Can I hold him?"

Ruth was not sure she heard what Mary said, so she simply nodded her head. Ruth washed the newborn baby with water and covered him with salt, an old tradition she had learned from the other midwives. The salt would help prevent infections on his tiny body. Ruth wrapped a cloth around the baby and gently placed the baby in Mary's arms.

Mary stared at the face of the tiny baby in awe. The baby's eyes were open, and he stared intently at his mother. There was an instant bond. He even smiled! Mary snuggled him close to her body and gently whispered in his ear, "Oh, Yeshua, you are so precious to me. I love you so much!" She gently rocked back and forth with Yeshua held close to her heart.

"He is healthy and perfect," Ruth said. "You look like you are doing well yourself. You don't need me anymore. I will leave you two alone with your new son. Do you have a name for him?" Ruth asked.

Joseph replied, "Yes, his name is Yeshua."

"Ahh, that is a good name; it means salvation," Ruth affirmed while nodding her head. "If you need anything, ask the innkeeper, and he will find me. There is a full moon out tonight, so I can walk home; it's not far."

After Ruth left, Mary and Joseph stared at Yeshua and then stared at each other. It was a holy moment as time stood still. The world faded away as they watched Yeshua, who was now sound asleep in Mary's arms. They had each been through so much in the past nine months; angelic visitations and dreams, doubts replaced by faith, fear replaced by hope. They now lived in a new world, a supernatural world where anything was possible. All because G-d came down from heaven to "tabernacle" with humanity through His son. The Feast of Tabernacles held a special meaning to them now.

"Joseph, please bring me that basket of cloths," Mary instructed. "I need to swaddle Yeshua like I have seen other mothers do. It will make him feel warm and secure."

Joseph brought the basket of cloths, and Mary took them out, one by one.

"These are special linen cloths which Elizabeth gave me," Mary shared as she slowly wrapped the cloths around Yeshua. "Elizabeth told me some of the priests at the Temple take their old garments and cut them into strips. The priests have reserved these linen cloths for years, waiting for the coming Messiah.

"And now, here he is! The angel told me, 'The holy one to be born will be called the Son of G-d.' The angel also said, 'The Lord G-d will give him the throne of his father David.' Now, here we are, in Bethlehem, the city where King David lived. Only G-d could arrange for all these things to happen!"[20]

"Yes, Mary, it is so amazing. Even though this is not an inn, we can use this manger as a safe place to lay Yeshua. There is already some hay in the manger, and I placed some of those extra cloths on top of the hay. This should make a soft bed for your son."

Joseph gently picked up Yeshua, who was completely swaddled with the priestly cloths. Joseph slowly placed him in the manger. Yeshua was sleeping and did not wake up during the short trip to his most unusual bed, a manger used for the Passover sheep.

Joseph sat down and stared at Yeshua. A tear slowly ran down his cheek. He wiped it away with one of the cloths. Mary looked at Joseph and asked, "Are you okay, Joseph?"

"Yes, yes, I am okay," Joseph replied, choking on the words. "It's overwhelming! I have never held a baby, yet here I am, responsible for this tiny, precious child... and responsible for you. I don't know why G-d choose me to be your husband."

---

[20] See prophecies 2, 10, and 12 in Prophecy Chart.

"Joseph, I know why," Mary spoke as she placed her hand on Joseph's arm. "You are a hard worker but gentle and kind. Moreover, you have a good heart. You will make a great provider for Yeshua and me. And you will teach him about his heavenly Father. G-d trusts you... and so do I."

Mary and Joseph both got close to the manger and silently stared at the sleeping baby. Yeshua had dark, slightly curly hair. Mary thought he was the most beautiful baby she had ever seen.

Baby Yeshua in the manger

Outside, on the road leading to the center of Bethlehem, Ruth walked quickly in the light of the moon. She kept thinking about the strange couple at the tower. She wondered if her eyes had deceived her. The light from the lantern was not the brightest, but she sure thought Mary was a virgin. How could that be? She remembered their holy scriptures prophesied the Messiah would be born of a virgin. But why would the Messiah be born in the Tower of the Flock, a place where the shepherds kept the Passover sheep? It did not make sense to her. Of course, the Hebrew Scriptures *did* say the Messiah would be born in Bethlehem. And here they were, in the town of Bethlehem.[21]

As Ruth walked home, she remembered the name of this newborn child—Yeshua. Ruth had been to Jerusalem many times for the Feast of Tabernacles. Everyone knew the Scriptures that were sung during this feast. As she walked home, she began to sing the ancient Psalm, "The Lord is my strength and my song, and he has become my yeshuah (salvation). Glad songs of yeshuah (salvation) are in the tabernacles of the righteous." She smiled when she reached the part about "yeshuah in the tabernacles of the righteous." It was almost as if this Feast was about *him*, the baby named Yeshua, who was born during the Feast of Tabernacles. She realized this was a night she would never forget.

---

[21] See prophecy 2 in Prophecy Chart.

Thought Provoking Journey:

- Mary sees the face of Yeshua (Jesus) after he is born. The Hebrew word for face is 'panim' and its form is plural. Why is this a plural word? Maybe it is because the Bible mentions the four faces of God?

- If Yeshua (Jesus) was born during the Feast of Tabernacles, it means:

  1. Yeshua was born when the people sing a song about 'yeshuah (salvation) is in the tabernacles of the righteous'.

  2. Yeshua was born during a feast which reminded the people of a time when God lived in their midst, in the wilderness Tabernacle.

  3. Yeshua was born during a feast which reminded the people when Solomon's Temple was dedicated. At that dedication, during this feast, the Shekinah presence of God came and dwelt in the Temple.

  4. Yeshua was born when the priests perform a water ceremony, which points to the coming of the future Messiah. This ceremony is in reference to Isaiah 44:3.

  5. Yeshua, the son of God, became flesh and lived among his people. (John 1:1-14)

  6. Yeshua was born during a feast when 'living' water was poured out at the Temple. Later, Jesus was associated with 'rivers of living water'. (John 7:37)

  7. Yeshua was born during a feast known for its magnificent light. Later, Jesus was known as the 'light of the world'. (John 8:12)

- All of the seven, annual Jewish feasts have prophetic implications. The Feast of Tabernacles is the last feast in the yearly cycle. Does this feast represent a future time when God will truly tabernacle (live) in the midst of his people in heaven?

- The story of the anointing of King Solomon can be found in the Bible in I Kings 1:32-45.

- The story of the birth of Yeshua (Jesus) can be found in the Bible in Matthew 1:18-25 and in Luke 2:1-7.

Chapter 9 Thoughts

Chapter 10
Firefall

On the first night of Sukkot, the night Yeshua was born, the shepherds from Bethlehem were staying out in the fields with their sheep. Since it was now fall, they were high up in the hills. It was too far to bring the sheep back to Bethlehem each night. Therefore, the shepherds kept watch over their flocks all night to prevent predators from attacking them.

Shepherd at night

There was a full moon shining in the sky, and a million stars twinkled brightly. The sheep had finally settled down to sleep. Josiah and Samuel were laying on their blankets, staring up into the sky. Jonathan was not with them this time. Rachel was pregnant and due in a couple of weeks. She had been having pains in her abdomen, so Jonathan decided to stay with her, in case she went into labor.

As the shepherds were preparing to go to sleep, a bright light appeared. A huge angel of the Lord was standing in front of the shepherds! The bright glory of G-d shone all around the angel, the sky was as bright as day. This terrified the shepherds! They had never seen such a light. They had heard about angelic visitations, but no one had ever seen an angel. This was a supernatural being and a supernatural experience.

The shepherds were frozen in fear, afraid to speak or move. Josiah stared at the angel and thought to himself, "What will the angel do; why is he here?"

The angel spoke to the group and said, "Fear not, for behold, I bring you good news of great joy that will be for all the people. For unto you is born this day in the city of David a Savior, who is Christ the Lord! And this will be a sign for you: you will find a baby wrapped in swaddling clothes and lying in a manger" (Luke 2:10–12).

As soon as he finished speaking, a large number of heavenly beings appeared with the angel. The "host of heaven" was in the sky, and they were all praising G-d! These supernatural beings were saying, "Glory to G-d in the highest, and on earth peace among those with whom he is pleased" (Luke 2:14).

Then, as quickly as the first angel had appeared, they all disappeared. They had returned to heaven. The shepherds all looked at each other in amazement. At first, no one spoke. Samuel finally spoke in awe, "Did everyone see the angels and hear what they said?"

Everyone started speaking at the same time and pointing to the sky. One shepherd said, "Those were angels; I am still shaking!" Another man blurted, "They said our Messiah has been born, here in Bethlehem."

A third shepherd exclaimed, "Yes, Bethlehem, the city of David, just as the prophets foretold!"

Josiah added, "They said we could find the baby wrapped in swaddling clothes and laying in a manger. This means he was born at the Tower of the Flock, where we swaddle our newborn sheep and put them in the manger. How odd is that?"

"Well, there is no room in the inns in Bethlehem because of the census. I guess it was the only place available for them," Samuel said. "Let's go to the Tower and see this baby."

The shepherds quickly walked down the hills to the Tower of the Flock. Thankfully, there was a full moon to help light their journey and it was a familiar path. However, the sky was brighter than normal. They came around a small hill and saw the Tower. Through the window, they could see someone was inside and had lit a lantern.

As they got closer to the Tower, they noticed another supernatural event in the sky. There was an extremely bright star, which moved slowly toward the Tower. Everyone stood still, wondering if they would see another angel.

Suddenly, the star stopped, right over the Tower. From the star, a stream of light began to emerge and flow toward the Tower. The white light turned reddish, orange, as if it were on fire. The light descended toward the top of the Tower, like a waterfall of fire. It seemed as if the star was dropping liquid fire on the Tower! When the stream of "fire" reached the tower, the fire spread out until the entire top of the Tower was covered with heavenly fire. Somehow, they all knew this was not a real fire.

Samuel spoke softly and said, "I think we are seeing seraphim, the holy angels of fire! The seraphim in heaven, worship Adonai continually."

Supernaturally, a fire from heaven had appeared as if to anoint the Tower of the Flock and its residents. As they watched, the liquid fire spilled from the top of the Tower and slowly ran down the side of the Tower. When the liquid fire reached the ground, it disappeared. The star still burned brightly, directly over the Tower.

The shepherds all stared at each other until someone said, "Let's go inside the tower and find the baby the angels told us about."

The shepherds walked to the tower and approached the door. Samuel knocked gently. A man slowly opened the door and stared at the shepherds. They peered inside and saw a young woman and a baby sleeping in the manger the shepherds use for the Passover sheep.

Samuel said, "Sir, we are shepherds, from Bethlehem. Tonight, we were watching our sheep, and an angel told us our long awaited Messiah has been born. The angel told us we would find the baby wrapped in swaddling clothes and laying in a manger. Is he here?"

Joseph opened the door and said, "Please, come in. Yes, here is the baby you seek. His name is Yeshua; he was born earlier tonight. His mother is sitting over there on the bed."

The shepherds crowded into the Tower of the Flock and nodded in respect to Mary. However, their eyes were on the baby, who woke up. Mary walked over, picked up Yeshua, and sat down, holding the baby so they could see his face. Yeshua opened his eyes and stared at the group of shepherds. Yeshua looked from one shepherd to the other, as if to look deep into their soul. Everyone knew it was a holy moment, and for a few minutes, no one spoke.

Samuel finally spoke, his voice shaking, "We all know the ancient prophecies about the Messiah and how he would be born in Bethlehem. Now, our eyes have seen the fulfillment of this ancient prophecy. We always wondered *who* the mother would be and *when* the Messiah would be born. But you are not from Bethlehem," Samuel said, turning to Mary and Joseph.

"No, we don't live in Bethlehem, but my ancestors are from this area," Joseph explained. "Herod's census required us to travel here from our hometown, even though she was pregnant. But now we understand she had to be here in Bethlehem to give birth, to fulfill the prophecy."

Samuel explained to Joseph everything the angel had said to them on the hillside. Joseph nodded his head, as if he understood supernatural events *could* truly take place.

Josiah looked at the manager and back to the baby. The infant was wrapped in swaddling clothes like the shepherds wrapped a Passover sheep when it was born. Josiah remembered when his beloved Chamoodi was born. His father wrapped the newborn lamb in cloths and placed him in *this same* manger.

"How odd," thought Josiah. "This baby was placed in the same manger as the Passover lamb." He remembered when Chamoodi was born, a fiery torch was taken to the roof of the tower, for the priests in Jerusalem to see. The fire would signify a lamb had been *certified* as a Passover sacrifice. And tonight they saw a supernatural fire on the roof of the Tower. "What could *that* mean?" Josiah pondered. It was all so mysterious.

Samuel knelt down before Yeshua in worship, and the other shepherds followed his example. The angels told them this baby was the Messiah. So Samuel spoke a blessing. "Baruch atah, Yeshua HaMashiach" (Blessed are you, Yeshua the Messiah). The shepherds softly and reverently repeated the same blessing to Yeshua. Josiah looked at Mary and noticed tears began to flow down her cheeks. She wiped them away with one hand, while cradling Yeshua in her other arm.

As the shepherds left the tower to walk back up the hill to their sheep, everyone spoke excitedly about this amazing night! They knew they would never forget the angels and their words. They knew G-d had finally fulfilled the age-old prophecy about their little town. They believed an eventful future lay ahead for them and the town of Bethlehem!

The following morning, a few shepherds stayed to guard the sheep, but most of them rushed down the ancient path to Bethlehem to share what they had seen during the night. They told everyone what the angels had said about the Messiah's birth. They shared how they found the baby, wrapped in swaddling clothes and laying in a manger, just as the angel had said. Everyone who heard their story was amazed at what the shepherds told them.

As Samuel shared the events from last night with his family, Jonathan shook his head and muttered, "I have never seen an angel, and I missed it last night." But in his heart, he knew he needed to be with his wife Rachel, during the night.

"Do not ever forget what has happened this day, in our town and in our lives," Samuel admonished his family as tears slowly ran down his face. "The Lord will keep every promise he has ever made. G-d is not a man that He should lie. Never forget that! Every promise spoken by His prophets will come to pass."

A holy silence fell over the entire family. Now that the Messiah had been born, they realized that Israel, maybe the entire world, would never be the same. Everything had changed... or would change when Yeshua became a man. There were many prophecies about the Messiah that could only be fulfilled when he became an adult. There was much more to anticipate when this child became a man.

Later that day, the shepherds returned to their sheep, praising G-d and giving Him the glory for all the things they had seen and heard. If anyone spoke about the angels or the baby, Samuel would start to cry. He could often be seen with his eyes closed, his hands raised in praise and tears streaming down his cheeks.

Josiah had never seen his father like this. And he *also* felt different inside. The experience of such an incredible supernatural event left a deep impression on his young soul.

Silently, Josiah prayed to Adonai, "May I never forget the wonderful things you have shown me. May I never forgot how it felt to see and hear the angels. And may I never forget you have truly sent the Messiah to be the Savior for our people. We have waited since ancient times for our Messiah. We have been on a very long journey, and the destination seemed so far away, we almost lost hope. The path has been long and hard, but now we see the end in sight. Our Messiah has finally arrived."

Because Rachel had been having abdominal pains, Jonathan was not with the shepherds when the angels announced the birth of Yeshua (Jesus). But he was still amazed the Messiah had finally been born in their hometown, according to the ancient prophecies. In addition, his own child would be born soon. He was praying for a son.

Meanwhile, Mary was amazed at the story that the shepherds shared. To think G-d would send angels to shepherds to announce the birth of Yeshua was stunning. Mary treasured all of these things in her heart and glorified the way G-d had worked everything out, exactly the way the Holy Scriptures had prophesied.

Mary pondered the events that had happened over the past year. Elizabeth, her relative, gave birth in her old age to a baby, which had been prophesied by an angel. In addition, Mary, while still a virgin, had conceived supernaturally, as prophesied by an angel. Now, she had given birth to a baby boy, as the angel had prophesied. And the shepherds heard angels share the announcement of her son's birth. She found herself living in a supernatural, spiritual world and wished everyone could have a supernatural encounter with G-d.

Mary and Joseph stayed at the Tower of the Flock for several days. Each morning, Joseph would walk to the local inn and purchase food and supplies for his family. Joseph also went to the authorities in Bethlehem and registered for the census, as required by Caesar Augustus. The news of the birth of Yeshua spread throughout Bethlehem. Everyone was talking about this child, whose birth was announced by an angelic host.

When Yeshua was eight days old, Joseph and Mary took Yeshua to Jerusalem to present him to the Lord, as was their custom. They went to the Temple and offered two birds as a sacrifice. It was also their custom that a male baby would be circumcised on the eighth day. In the Jewish tradition, the number eight stood for a new beginning and for dedication to G-d. The world was created by G-d in six days, and he rested on the seventh day. The eighth day was the beginning of the new week, a new beginning. Years earlier, after Antiochus Epiphanies defiled the

Holy Temple, the rededication of the Temple took eight days. The eighth day marked a new beginning between the Jewish people and their G-d, as they rededicated their lives to their Creator. The Feast of Tabernacles lasted for seven days but ended with a day of celebration on the eighth day.

In the Jewish tradition, a baby was officially given his name on the eighth day. Therefore, this day, her baby would be circumcised and officially given his name—Yeshua, which meant "salvation." Mary remembered what the angel of G-d told her when she conceived. The angel said, "The holy one to be born will be called the Son of G-d." This was truly the beginning of a new age; G-d wrapped himself in human flesh and became a man. She thought, "How wonderful we can have a relationship with G-d, through his son, Yeshua." She wondered what Yeshua would do and say when he became a man. Maybe they could learn more about the heart of G-d and what would truly please him.

There was an old man living in Jerusalem named Simeon, who performed circumcisions. He was a devout and righteous man, waiting for the promise of the Messiah. Earlier, the Holy Spirit of G-d had revealed to Simeon that he would not see death until he first saw the Messiah. The Holy Spirit directed him to come to the Temple on the day that Mary and Joseph brought Yeshua. When Mary and Joseph brought Yeshua to Simeon to perform the circumcision, Simeon took the baby in his arms. By the Spirit, Simeon knew Yeshua was the Messiah. He blessed G-d and said, "Lord, now you are letting your servant depart in peace, according to your word; for my eyes have seen your salvation that you have prepared in the presence of all peoples, a light for revelation to the Gentiles, and for glory to your people Israel" (Luke 2:29–32).

Mary and Joseph were amazed this stranger knew Yeshua was the Messiah! Only G-d could have revealed this information to a total stranger. Simeon circumcised the baby, according to the Law. He blessed them and said to Mary, "Behold, this Child is destined for the fall and rising of many in Israel. But a sword will also pierce through your own soul." When Simeon was finished, he handed Yeshua back to Mary and

Joseph. Mary wondered what he meant by "a sword will pierce your soul," but she was too timid to ask Simeon.

There was also an 84-year-old prophetess who lived at the Temple complex. Her name was Anna, and she was widowed at a young age, after only 7 years of marriage. Now, she spent her time at the Temple, serving G-d by praying and fasting often. Anna came into the Temple area and when she saw Yeshua, she *also* recognized he was the Messiah! She praised G-d that He had answered the prayers of generations. Simeon and Anna both knew they had seen the Messiah. The Holy Scriptures say in the mouth of two or three witnesses that everything is established. So, G-d had two witnesses at the Temple to confirm, by the Spirit, that Yeshua was the Messiah.

Mary and Joseph left Jerusalem and returned to Bethlehem. By now, most of the travelers to Bethlehem had returned to their own town, after they registered for the census. However, Joseph did not want Mary to travel all the way to Nazareth since she gave birth a week earlier. Therefore, he asked around and found a vacant home where he and his family could live. He decided to keep his family in Bethlehem for a while. The townspeople welcomed them warmly. Joseph was a stonemason and a carpenter. He was quickly able to find work with some of the local people.

After their exciting encounter with the angels, the shepherds continued to watch their sheep out in the fields for a few more weeks. About two weeks after Yeshua was born, Rachel went into labor and delivered a healthy baby boy. Jonathan named him Reuben. It was the first grandchild for Josiah's parents, but they hoped for many more. Since they all lived in the same house together, everyone was excited to have a new baby in the house.

Because Bethlehem was a small town, everyone knew all of the residents and where they lived. By now, the townspeople knew Joseph and Mary, along with Yeshua, had moved into one of the vacant houses in Bethlehem. Josiah thought it would be exhilarating to watch Yeshua and Reuben grow up together.

A few weeks after Reuben was born, Josiah was with the shepherds up on the hillside, watching the sheep. In a few weeks, they would bring all of the sheep down the hills to spend the winter in town. On this night, Josiah was sleeping outside with the men. While Josiah slept, he had another dream. A year earlier, Josiah had a dream where he heard the melody of a simple song. The words of that song were "I know there's more than what teachers are teaching, I know there's so much more."

Now, a year later, he had another dream very similar to the first dream. In the second dream, Josiah again heard someone singing the *same* melody with the words from the first dream. After the song was sung through the first time, he heard the same melody but now with different words. This time, the song continued: "I know there's more than what *angels are singing*, yes there's so much more." The entire song was sung three times, and Josiah woke up.

Josiah felt a chill run down his back. He felt as if he was in the presence of angels again, but he did not *see* any angels. He thought about the words in the song, the words that stated there was something more to know than what the angels were singing. He remembered the night when Yeshua was born, and he remembered the angels in the sky. The angel said, "For unto you is born this day in the city of David a Savior, who is Christ the Lord."

Now, the song in his dream stated there is more than the fact the Messiah had been born. Josiah pondered what this could mean. "There is more than the angels are singing?" He wondered, "Did this second dream have a hidden message about the *life* of Yeshua?" He was glad Yeshua lived in Bethlehem, where *he* lived. As Yeshua grew up, Josiah was planning to watch his life and see what happened with Israel's long-awaited Messiah.

Josiah was now 10 years old and learning much from their Holy Scriptures. He remembered a portion of Scripture that he had read recently. The scripture was in Isaiah 49:6; G-d is speaking and talking about restoring the tribes of Jacob and bringing them back to Israel. In this passage, G-d says, "I will make you as a light for the nations that my salvation may reach to the ends of the earth." Josiah wondered what being "a light for the nations" meant and how does a person "take G-d's salvation to the ends of the earth."

Josiah did not understand what this scripture meant. Even the learned rabbis could not agree on the meaning of this scripture. He remembered another scripture in Daniel 2:28 that states, "There is a G-d in heaven who reveals mysteries." His dream made him realize that sometimes, only G-d can reveal the mysteries that are hidden in His scriptures and therefore unveil their meaning.

As Josiah drifted back to sleep, he could hear the simple melody in his head, and it brought him comfort. "There must be a reason why G-d has given me these dreams," he thought. He prayed and asked Adonai to help him to learn the mysteries hidden within the Holy Scriptures and within his dreams. He also knew these mysteries were associated with the baby Yeshua. To see the body of baby Yeshua, you had to first unwrap each layer of swaddling clothes, one at a time.

The prophetic mysteries were words wrapped around the promise of the Messiah, like the swaddling clothes that wrapped Yeshua. Josiah believed that as each prophecy was fulfilled, one at a time, Yeshua would be recognized as the Messiah. This would happen during the lifetime of Yeshua, as the words in his dream proclaimed. "I know there's more than what angels are singing, yes there's so much more," he said to himself.

"Yes," Josiah thought, "I know there is much more to come! I will watch this child grow up and watch the unwrapping and fulfillment of the ancient, mysterious prophecies."

Thought Provoking Journey:

- There are over 100 prophecies in the Hebrew Bible (the Tanakh or Old Testament) about the birth and life of the promised Messiah of Israel.

- The Spirit of God can reveal, to an individual, what has been hidden in scripture. God can also use dreams and visions to reveal Himself to those who seek him.

- When Yeshua was born, a supernatural light (a star) appeared over the place where he was born. When a Passover sheep was born, a torch was taken to the top of the tower to announce the birth. The star, in essence, announced the birth of the new born lamb of God.

- One of the messages of the Bible is that ordinary people, had supernatural encounters, with God or his angels. These encounters changed the destiny of the person, his descendants and sometimes entire nations.

  - Noah - God told him to build an ark even though it had never rained.
  - Abraham - God told him to leave where he lived, for a place God would show him.
  - Jacob - Had a dream and saw angels coming down and going up to heaven.
  - Joseph - Had a dream that he would be a ruler one day.
  - Moses - Had a 'burning bush' encounter when God spoke to him.
  - Isaiah - Had a vision and saw God 'high and lifted up' in heaven and gave many prophecies about the Messiah.
  - Elijah - Was taken by a whirlwind into heaven, without dying.

- In the Bible, God is sometimes described as fire. The prophet Ezekiel has a vision of God sitting on the throne. He states that from His waist down, God appeared as fire. (Ezekiel 1:27)

- Seraphim are a special class of angels who are associated with fire and burning; their focus is to worship God and serve in His presence.

- A supernatural experience which is from God, will align with the Word of God. It will never contradict the Word of God, nor the character of God.

Chapter 10 Thoughts

Chapter 11

Treasures We Bring

◄··──────── ❦ ────────··►

W hen Yeshua was born in Bethlehem, there were several wise
men living in another country east of Israel. These men understood the prophecies about the Jewish Messiah. Previously, they read
Daniel 9 about the "seventy sevens" and, according to their calculations,
they believed the time had come for the Messiah to be born. So they
were looking for a supernatural sign.

On the night Yeshua was born, these wise men were searching the
skies and saw a very bright star; they knew it was *his* star.[22] They knew
the Messiah had been born, and according to the prophecies, they
knew he would be the King of Israel. Since the winter rains would be
coming soon, they planned to leave for Jerusalem in the spring. It was
a long way to travel, and it might take a couple of years to reach Israel,
because of the weather. However, they determined to make the long
trip to Israel, in search of the child they knew had been born. Their
journey would take them on an ancient path to Jerusalem, and maybe
beyond. Their journey was to find the Messiah.

---

[22] See prophecy 13 in Prophecy Chart.

Wise men

Meanwhile, in Bethlehem, life for Joseph, Mary, and Yeshua had settled down into a routine. After the Feast of Tabernacles was over, the weather turned cold and rainy, and the town slowly settled down for the winter. Mary and Joseph were living in the house that Joseph located earlier. Joseph continued to find work, sometimes as a stonemason and sometimes as a carpenter. Mary spent her time caring for her newborn son, preparing the meals, and taking care of the house. They made friends with the local residents and attended the synagogue, in Bethlehem, every Sabbath. Several other women had babies near the age of Yeshua, so Mary adapted to her new hometown and quickly made friends.

The story of how the angels appeared to the local shepherds was well known, and everyone in the area believed Yeshua was indeed the Messiah. Mary and Joseph were shown great respect because of this perception.

The weeks turned into months, and the annual feasts started over again. In the spring, the three Passover feasts were celebrated (Passover, Unleavened Bread, First Fruits), followed by Shavuot (Pentecost). In the fall, Rosh HaShana (Head of the Year) and Yom Kippur (Day of Atonement) were celebrated, followed by Sukkot (Feasts of

Tabernacles). Life for the shepherds followed the same annual pattern. Baby lambs were born in the spring. Summer came, and the sheep foraged the nearby meadows and streams for food. When the summer harvest was over, the sheep traveled further up the hillside until the weather turned cold and the sheep came back to town for the winter.

Jonathan and Rachel's son, Reuben, grew and after a few months, he was crawling and finally walking. Josiah enjoyed playing with him and being silly. Josiah would make funny faces or noises, and Reuben would make a big belly laugh, while the entire family watched and laughed with him. Reuben was a happy and plump baby. He often followed Josiah around the house, babbling and grabbing at everything in his reach.

Josiah had to be careful with his lyre. He always placed it up very high so Reuben could not touch it. He did not want his lyre to get broken again. Josiah had learned to play and sing quite well. When he had time to relax, he would sometimes play the strings, and a melody would come to his mind. Words would flow to match the melody. Everyone said he had a talent to play, just like David.

Every time Josiah walked past the house where Mary and Joseph lived, he would glance through the open door or window. He would sometimes see Yeshua and his mom playing the same silly games he played with Reuben. Every time he saw Yeshua, he would remember the night the angels announced his birth. And he would always feel a slight shiver go down his back. Not a shiver of fear but a shiver of awe and a feeling he was in the presence of angels again.

After the birth of Yeshua, when the Feast of Tabernacles came again, the shepherds all recounted their experience from the previous year. The rabbi at their local synagogue would often ask them questions about the angels they saw that night and the baby they found at the Tower with his parents. Amazement and awe would once again fill their hearts to know the Messiah had been born in Bethlehem, in fulfillment of the Hebrew Scriptures. The Feast of Tabernacles was a joyous weeklong celebration. It was almost as if they were celebrating the birth of Yeshua!

Mary and Joseph had now lived in Bethlehem for a year. Mary hoped they would eventually return to Nazareth and live in their old hometown. But, for now, Bethlehem was a safe place to live and work. Mary often thought about all the prophetic words that had been spoken about the Messiah, and she wondered when and how they would be fulfilled.

Winter came again, and when it was over, everyone planned their lives around the spring feasts, which would start soon. The cadence of their life flowed around the weekly Sabbaths, the annual feasts, and the agricultural activities that took place during each season.

In the summer before Yeshua was almost two years old, the wise men from the east finally arrived in Jerusalem, the capital of Israel. The entourage of the men, their servants and camels, made its way through the streets of Jerusalem and went the Herod's palace for an audience with the king. Herod, the King of Israel, whom they now called Herod the Great, lived in a grand palace in Jerusalem. The wise men entered the palace and approached Herod with great reverence.

"Why have you come to Jerusalem, from so far away?" Herod asked.

One of the men asked, "Where is the one who has been born king of the Jews? We saw his star when it rose, and we have come to worship him."

Herod replied, "What is this you speak of, a baby who is king of the Jews? I am King of the Jews—and the King of all Israel! I do not have a newborn son."

"A child has been born," one of the men said. "He will be the Messiah of Israel. We have seen His star."

Herod could barely contain his rage. He would *not* allow anyone to take away his throne! He had already murdered three of his own sons who were a threat to his kingdom.

"Let me consult with our teachers and prophets and see if they know where this child has been born," Herod said. "I will let you know what they tell me."

The wise men left the palace, assured that King Herod would be able to help them determine the city where they should look for this child. However, Herod was livid! Word spread quickly through Jerusalem, and everyone was disturbed. Herod had a reputation as a violent and ruthless leader.

Herod called for the most learned chief priests and rabbis, the teachers of the law. He asked them, "Where do the Hebrew scriptures say the Messiah will be born?"

"In Bethlehem, in Judea," they replied, "for this is what the prophet has written, 'But you, Bethlehem, in the land of Judah, are by no means least among the rulers of Judah; for out of you will come a ruler who will shepherd my people Israel.'"[23]

Herod called for the wise men and shared his findings. "According to our rabbis, the child was born in Bethlehem. Go and search carefully for the child," Herod instructed them. "As soon as you find him, report back to me so I may also go and worship him." Herod also found out from them, the exact time the star appeared. He had no intention to worship this baby. He had other plans.

The wise men left Jerusalem later that afternoon and traveled to Bethlehem, which was only five miles away. When night came, the star they had seen earlier rose in the sky and went ahead of them. They made their way to Bethlehem, following the star with joy.

As they entered the little town of Bethlehem, the townspeople heard this large caravan, and people began to look out their windows to see what was happening. These men were dressed like royalty. They had many camels and servants as well. They were astonished to see these visitors in their town.

---

[23] See prophecy 2 in Prophecy Chart.

Jonathan noticed the caravan as it moved past their window and called to everyone, "Look, a caravan. They are not from around here. Look at their robes and turbans; it looks like they are from the east, maybe Persia."

"Why are they here?" Josiah asked.

"I don't know," Jonathan replied. "Maybe they are on their way to Egypt. They came from the direction of Jerusalem."

Jonathan closed the window and headed back to his side of the house. But Josiah was curious. As the caravan passed his house, he slowly opened the door and slipped outside, without anyone noticing. He followed the caravan from a distance. He noticed a large star ahead of the caravan. The bright star gave enough light to travel safely.

The star stopped over the house where Mary, Joseph, and Yeshua now lived. The caravan of camels stopped, and the men dismounted. Mary had opened the window to see what was causing so much noise. When Mary saw the caravan with the wise men and their servants, she quickly grabbed Yeshua and held him tight. She did not know what to expect. Who were these strangers, and what did they want? She called for Joseph as she watched through the window.

Joseph opened the door to their home and anxiously stared at the men. One of the wise men bowed toward them and said, "Do not be afraid, for we know your child is the Messiah of Israel. We have come from far away to worship him. We have studied the ancient Hebrew prophecies about the Messiah for years. Therefore, we knew it was time for him to come. When he was born, we saw his star, and we traveled to Jerusalem to find him."

Joseph motioned for the men to come into their small home. He left the door open because there was not enough room for everyone to come inside. Three of the men were dressed extravagantly and were the leaders of this group. These three men came into the house and bowed down before Mary, where she was sitting with Yeshua on her lap.

Each man motioned for his servant to bring forth the gifts that he had brought. One by one, a servant brought to Mary a costly gift and placed it at her feet. They brought gifts fitting for a king.

One man placed a large bowl of frankincense at Mary's feet, along with another bag full of this expensive resin. A second man placed a large box at Mary's feet. He opened it to display a large quantity of expensive myrrh. Still another man presented Mary with bag of gold coins! Mary had never seen so much gold in all her life; it was a fortune.

Mary and Joseph did not know what to say, they could not believe their eyes! The wise men shared how they traveled from the east to Jerusalem, looking for the King and Messiah of Israel. They explained they stopped to ask King Herod where the new king was born.

When they mentioned King Herod, Mary held Yeshua even tighter. The leader of the group told Mary that King Herod wanted to also come and worship her son. When Mary heard this, she looked up at Joseph. Her eyes were full of fear and dread. Joseph gently put his hand on Mary's shoulder and drew her closer to his side, as if to show he would protect her and Yeshua.

Josiah had followed the caravan to the house where Mary and Joseph lived. He hid quietly behind the corner of a building and watched as the servants brought gifts into the house. Without being seen, he made his way to an open window and watched as the enormous treasure was presented, in worship, to Yeshua. Josiah was in awe once again, like the night when he saw the angels and heard the announcement of the birth of Yeshua.

When Josiah saw the men were ready to leave, he silently made his way back to his house. He quietly entered his home and decided he would not mention what he saw to anyone.

"Yeshua *must* be the Messiah!" he thought once again. Of course, he never doubted what the angels had told the shepherds when Yeshua was born. But tonight was another supernatural occurrence which confirmed once again, what the angels had announced almost two years ago. He remembered what his father always said, "Adonai, our G-d, never lies!"

Josiah thought about the gifts of gold, frankincense, and myrrh. A few days earlier, on the Day of Atonement, his father had explained these three items were part of the rituals and elements of worship to Adonai at the Holy Temple. He thought it was riveting that these were the gifts brought to Yeshua. He wondered if there was some other hidden meaning to these gifts. Maybe it simply meant the wise men worshipped Yeshua with the same items used to worship G-d in the Holy Temple. He was only 12 years old, but mysteries like this intrigued him.

The wise men decided to stay at one of the inns in Bethlehem and rest before returning home. That night, the leader of the wise men had a dream. In the dream, an angel told him they must *not* go back to Jerusalem to talk with Herod. The angel warned him it was a trap and they should return to their own country a different way. The next morning, the caravan headed out of Bethlehem going in a direction *away* from Jerusalem before heading back to their home country.

That same night, Joseph also had a dream. An angel of the Lord appeared to Joseph and said, "Get up, take the child and his mother and escape to Egypt. Stay there until I tell you, for Herod is going to search for the child to kill him."

Joseph immediately arose and woke up Mary. He explained G-d had warned him in a dream to flee to Egypt. They packed up their belongings and the gifts from the wise men. They loaded two donkeys and prepared to leave the place they had called home for almost two years. Joseph placed a couple of gold coins on the table for the landlord and they quietly rode off in the night.

Mary's voice shook as she asked Joseph, "Where will we go? We don't know anyone in Egypt."

"There are many Jewish people in Egypt. In fact, the Zadok priest Onias ordered the Essenes to build another temple near Memphis, over

100 years ago. It is in Leontopolis; we should travel to that city. Surely, we will find some righteous Jewish people there, who believe in the one true G-d."

Yeshua was sleeping in Mary's arms as she hugged him close to her chest. Tears began to flow down her cheeks as they traveled the path toward Egypt. She had tears of gratitude to Adonai for preserving the life of Yeshua. The gifts left by the wise men were so valuable, they could live many years in Egypt. She marveled at G-d's provision and timing. In addition, she remembered another prophecy that had been spoken about the Messiah. Through the prophet Hosea, G-d said, "Out of Egypt I called my son"[24] (Hosea 11:1).

The next morning, Josiah decided he could not keep his secret any longer. While the family was eating breakfast, he finally blurted out, "I know why the camel caravan came to Bethlehem."

"What do you mean?" his father inquired. "How would *you* know such a thing?"

"I followed the camels last night to see where they were going. They went to the home of Joseph and Mary and little Yeshua," Josiah explained with excitement.

"A star led them directly to the house. They went inside to worship Yeshua! They knew he was the Messiah, and they gave him gifts, expensive gifts," he continued.

"Josiah, were you listening to their conversation?" Samuel asked sternly.

"Yes, I know it was not the right thing to do, but it was so exciting to see such great and rich men," Josiah continued.

"How did they know to come to Bethlehem?" Jonathan asked.

"I heard one of them say they went to King Herod's palace. The night Yeshua was born, they saw a bright star. They had studied our ancient Scriptures and knew it was a sign of the Messiah's birth. It was the same star we saw over the Tower of the Flock. They knew the King

---

[24] See prophecy 14 in Prophecy Chart.

of the Jews had been born. They thought King Herod would know the location of his birth," Josiah replied.

"King Herod!" bellowed Jonathan. "That filthy piece of humanity! He is not fit to be the king of Israel; he is a power-hungry politician!"

"Jonathan, calm down," Samuel implored sternly. "Come, we need to take care of the sheep." The men arose from the table and headed for the door. Before he left, Josiah ran over to Reuben and tickled him on his stomach. Reuben burst out in squeals of joy while everyone laughed at the sight of the two boys playing with each other.

Josiah grabbed his lyre and quickly followed his father and Jonathan out the door and toward the sheep. Since it was summer, the sheep stayed in the pens at night. This morning, the shepherds would lead the sheep to a new pasture not far away and return home at night. It seems that nothing could stop the rhythm of life in Bethlehem. It was the way of the shepherd.

Thought Provoking Journey:

- It is possible that the wise men were living in Persia (Babylon), which is east of Bethlehem. Several hundred years earlier, the Jewish people were taken to Babylon and into captivity, after their country was taken over by the Babylonian empire. Educated Jewish men living in Babylon (men like Daniel, Shadrach, Meshach and Abendigo), knew about the prophecies concerning the birth of the Messiah. Seventy years after their captivity, many Jews returned to Israel, but some stayed in Babylon, because they had established a business. The wise men who searched for Yeshua, were probably descendants of the Jewish people who stayed in Babylon, hundreds of years earlier.

- The wise men brought gold, frankincense and myrrh, as gifts to Yeshua. It is interesting to note that the only place in the Bible where all three of these items are mentioned, is in reference to the Temple, where God dwelt and where He was worshipped.

  - Gold was used extensively in the Temple. The Ark of the Covenant was made from pure gold. The walls inside the Temple were covered with gold and most of the elements, used in the Temple, were made from gold.

  - Frankincense is a resin which comes from a tree, similar to turpentine. It was burned for its pleasant fragrance when animals were sacrificed, in the courtyard of the Temple.

  - Myrrh was the first ingredient used to make the incense which was offered on the Altar of Incense inside the Temple.

- The story of the wise men can be found in the Bible, in Matthew 2:1-12.

www.ngcarraway.com

Chapter 11 Thoughts

Chapter 12
The Wrath of Herod

In Jerusalem, King Herod anxiously waited for the wise men to report back to him. A couple of weeks passed, but the wise men had not returned. King Herod realized the wise men had outwitted him. He was furious! He knew they went to the town of Bethlehem in search of the child. Herod calculated the child was under two years of age, based on the time the wise men saw the star. His sinister mind began to contemplate his next course of action.

Meanwhile, in Bethlehem, life returned to normal for the shepherds. Josiah took his lyre with him almost everywhere he went. Josiah would sing the songs he heard in his dreams. When he sang the song called "I Know There's More," a discussion would always follow about the meaning of the song. He would also make up simple songs about life in Bethlehem. The other shepherds enjoyed his playing and singing; it helped to pass the time when they were up on the hills.

One morning, Jonathan and Josiah were at the sheep pen, and Jonathan noticed a small sheep that was sick. He prepared a place for the little sheep to stay in the pen and made sure there was water nearby. He and Josiah then headed up the hill with their father and the other shepherds. They led the sheep to a new pasture that was not far from the main road. After lunch, the shepherds noticed a group of men riding towards Bethlehem from Jerusalem. They were dressed like soldiers but not Roman soldiers.

"Those men look like Herod's soldiers," Jonathan snorted with disdain. "Why are they headed to Bethlehem? Maybe they are on their way to Herod's temple at Masada."

Jonathan turned to Josiah and said, "Why don't you come with me? I want to go check on Rachel; she has not been feeling well lately. Maybe you can play with Reuben for a little while. And I need to check on the sick lamb in the pen, too."

"Father, we will return in a few minutes," Jonathan explained to Samuel. "Rachel has been sick every morning for the past few weeks."

Samuel smiled and nodded his head, as if he knew a secret. "Go my son, check on your wife."

Josiah laid his lyre down next to his father, and he and Jonathan started walking down the hill to Bethlehem, not far away.

"Look, Jonathan, over there, coming from Jerusalem. Those are the soldiers we saw earlier," Josiah exclaimed.

Jonathan gazed in the direction where Josiah was pointing. "Yes, they *are* Herod's soldiers, not Roman soldiers. They are headed towards Bethlehem. That is strange; Herod has never shown interest in Bethlehem."

They both picked up their pace so they would reach Bethlehem soon after the soldiers, anxious to see why soldiers would visit their peaceful town.

"Josiah, go to the house and tell Rachel I will be there soon. I need to stop by the pen and check on the sick lamb, and then I will come home," Jonathan instructed his brother.

Josiah quickly walked toward his home, but he was not prepared for what happened next. Before he reached his home, he heard a woman scream and a baby crying. Down the street, he could see

Herod's soldiers pushing their way into one house after another. There were shouts and screams coming from different directions.

"What is happening?" Josiah wondered as a sense of fear and dread swept over him. He ran toward his house, passing several homes where he could hear the angry shouts of the soldiers and the cries of women.

He pushed the front door open and called out, "Rachel, where are you? Mom! Hannah!"

Rachel appeared in a doorway, holding Reuben on her hip. "What is it, Josiah? What is happening?"

"There are soldiers here, Herod's soldiers came—"

A large soldier burst through the front door of their home, with a sword in his hand. Josiah's mother and sister appeared from a back room and screamed.

As the soldier approached Rachel, she started backing up toward the wall, holding Reuben tightly. The soldier reached out and grabbed Rachel's arm as she struggled to pull away.

"Stop! Get out!" Josiah shouted at the man, as he ran toward him, even though the man was twice his size. Josiah's mother and sister also ran toward the man to try to stop his violent actions. The soldier released Rachel so he could push Josiah's mother and Hannah to the floor, knocking furniture over as he pushed them. With his other arm, he easily shoved Josiah backward. Josiah tripped and fell over, hitting his head. As he got up, he felt warm blood running down his face.

Josiah's mother lay unconscious on the floor as Hannah huddled behind her mother's motionless body, wailing uncontrollably.

The soldier reached toward Rachel again, but this time, he grabbed Reuben and wrestled the baby out of Rachel's arms. Reuben was bawling and thrashing his arms and legs around. The soldier kicked Rachel in the stomach so hard she fell backward to the floor. The soldier raised his sword.

"Josiah, get Jonathan!" Rachel shouted, holding her stomach.

Josiah stumbled to the door but glanced back to see Rachel's robe covered in blood from the waist down. Little Reuben had a terrified look in his eyes as he frantically searched for his mother. Just before he ran out of the house, Josiah saw the sword swing down towards Reuben. He heard Rachel scream, "Noooo!"

As he ran out of the house, he heard Reuben's loud shrieks and Rachel's screams, and suddenly, Reuben's cries were silenced.

Josiah ran as fast as he could down the street, but he could already see Jonathan racing toward him. When they reached each other, Jonathan grabbed Josiah by the shoulders. "You are bleeding! What is happening?"

Josiah could hardly breathe but he blurted out, "It's Rachel, she needs you. And the solider has Rueben and, and, and he has a sword!"

Jonathan took off at a full run toward his house, which was not far down the street. Josiah turned around to sprint after him.

When the door to their home came into view, they both saw a soldier walking out, sword in hand. He deftly held the sword straight out and turned it to the left, then to the right, letting blood drip off his sword onto the dusty street. As Jonathan charged toward him, a primal scream came out of Jonathan's throat. The look in Jonathan's eyes was pure rage.

Jonathan, the gentle shepherd with no weapon, was no match for the soldier, who was trained for battle. As Jonathan ran, he lowered his head and tried to knock the man over by butting his head into the soldier's chest. The soldier braced himself and turned slightly to his left when Jonathan plowed into him. Jonathan lost his balance and fell to his right. The soldier quickly swung his sword toward Jonathan's left leg and landed a blow on Jonathan's bare leg.

Jonathan fell to the ground as blood gushed from a gash on his leg. Josiah reached Jonathan and helped him stand up. The soldier grunted like an animal and strode away.

Josiah helped Jonathan as he limped through the door of their home. They both stopped in their tracks when they saw what lay ahead. Rachel was sitting on the floor with her back against the wall; her legs were stretched straight out. She was weeping as she held Reuben in her arms and gently rocked him back and forth. She was covered in blood. Reuben's head was at an odd angle. His eyes were wide open, but there was no light in his eyes. Reuben was dead.

When Jonathan realized what had happened to his son, his first-born son, he let out a sound that came from deep inside his soul. A terrifying sound Josiah had never heard before. Jonathan stumbled to where Rachel sat with Reuben and fell to his knees. He gently picked up Reuben's lifeless body and tried to place his little head in the proper position on his little body. But Reuben's head would not stay in the correct position, it simply flopped over. Reuben lay in Jonathan's bloody hands, which were now shaking. The tears from Jonathan's eyes splattered on little Reuben's body, mixing with the blood and making little pink rivers on the baby's clothes. Rachel's hands were held at her mouth, as her body heaved in waves of despair. She slowly fell sideways, her hands dropping as she became unconscious. Her face now showed the bloody imprint of her hands; it was a ghastly scene.

Josiah had never seen such anguish. His entire body began to spasm, and it felt as if his stomach flipped upside down. He had never felt so helpless or so hopeless. His mother had regained consciousness and sat next to Hannah, her arms tightly wrapped around her daughter. Hannah was weeping uncontrollably with a portion of her robe covering her eyes, as if to block out the horrific view before her. Josiah's mother was heaving and gasping for breath, unable to comprehend what had happened in her home.

Josiah could not believe what he was seeing. How could this happen, in such a short span of time? He noticed Jonathan's left leg was bleeding profusely, so he found a cloth and tied it around Jonathan's leg.

Everyone was in a daze. The image of Jonathan holding his limp son was burned in Josiah's mind. Josiah heard shouts outside and went to see what was happening. There were multitudes of villagers in the streets. People were crying and shouting at the soldiers, as they left Bethlehem, headed back to Jerusalem. Josiah ran to a group of people, and he heard a woman say, "They told us they were looking for all the baby boys who were two years of age and younger. He said they had orders from Herod to kill all of the boys born here in the past two years. Why would Herod do such a thing?"

Josiah remembered the wise men told Mary and Joseph that Herod had inquired about the time when they saw the star. The men told Herod the star appeared almost two years earlier, when the Messiah was born. Suddenly, Josiah realized what had happened. Herod was trying to kill Yeshua, the baby who had been born King of the Jews!

His heart was pounding as he raced to the house where Mary and Joseph lived with Yeshua. When he reached the house, he did not even knock. He threw open the door and shouted, "Mary, Joseph, Yeshua!"

He glanced around the little house and noticed there was nothing in the house. It was vacant. "How did this happen?" he wondered. "I saw them a few days ago, when the men came with their treasures."

He was perplexed, so he walked down the street toward his home. In the midst of the chaos and confusion, he saw the man who owned the house, where Mary and Joseph had been staying. Josiah went up to the man and asked, "Did you know Mary and Joseph are gone? Their house is empty."

"Why, yes, I knew. I went by the house a couple of days ago, and they were not there. On the table were two gold coins! Can you believe it? There was a note that said I should keep the gold as payment for their rent. Joseph said they had to leave unexpectedly. But he paid me much more than what he owed me. I wonder where they went. Maybe back to their hometown. It seems they left at a good time."

Josiah pondered what he had heard. Somehow, Adonai had warned Mary and Joseph, and they left Bethlehem to avoid Herod's murderous rage. He was relieved Yeshua had not been killed. Adonai had miraculously saved the Messiah of Israel, the one who was destined to save Israel.

He turned and saw his father and the other shepherds coming into town. They had heard the noise and the screams, even up on the hillside. Josiah raced over to his father and buried his head in his father's chest, sobbing and shaking.

"Josiah, what has happened? I see people injured and bleeding. And some of the women are wailing as if someone has died."

"Father, Herod's soldiers came in search of Yeshua! They killed all of the baby boys under two years of age."

Samuel pulled Josiah away from his chest and looked him straight in the face. "Boys under two years of age? What about Reuben?"

Josiah could not speak; he could only shake his head as he sobbed violently, his whole body convulsing. Samuel saw the look on Josiah's face, and no words were needed. At the instant of understanding, Samuel almost collapsed, but Josiah caught him.

"Adonai!" Samuel shrieked, "Have mercy!"

It seemed as if Samuel had aged 20 years in an instant. He doubled over, clutching his chest and breathing very heavy. He could hardly walk. Josiah helped his father stumble the short distance to their home.

When they entered the house, Samuel's eyes went directly to Jonathan, who was sitting on the floor, still trying to hold Reuben's head in the correct position. Jonathan did not say a word but shook his head slowly while tears ran down his face and he sobbed uncontrollably. The cloth around his leg was soaked in blood, as was his robe.

Samuel grabbed the top of this robe and tore it from top to bottom, the ancient sign of sorrow. A sound came forth from his mouth that no one had ever heard. It was the sound of unbearable anguish and grief. It came from his innermost being. Everyone in the house was weeping from the deep heartbreak of losing this innocent baby. Their cries joined the chorus of pain and agony heard from several homes, in the little town of Bethlehem. Their grief made a mournful chorus that hung over the town like a dark fog.

Samuel staggered toward Jonathan. With tear-filled eyes, everyone watched Samuel, the patriarch of their family as he approached Jonathan. Samuel knelt on the floor next to Jonathan and reached for the child. With shaking arms, Jonathan handed Reuben's lifeless body to his father. Samuel gently cradled Reuben's body in his arms. The tears flowed freely down the wrinkles in his face, as he held the body of Reuben and slowly rocked him back and forth.

By this time, several neighbors had arrived and quietly entered the house. The women surrounded Rachel, Hannah, and Josiah's mother, trying to comfort them. The men stood reverently, inside the door, but even these strong men could not hold back their tears. It seemed as if hours passed with no one moving.

Eventually, Samuel lifted little Reuben's body up toward heaven, and he slowly said, "Adonai gave this precious child to our family. Now, he sleeps. We will see him again in the resurrection."

Rachel tried to stand up, but she had lost so much blood she collapsed on the floor. The women from the neighborhood helped her as she struggled to stand and walk toward the back of the house, where she and Jonathan lived.

Josiah's mother stood up, and Samuel gently handed Reuben's body to her. She took a nearby cloth and wrapped it around Reuben until the entire body was covered. She gently kissed the fabric that covered the top of Reuben's head as she left the gathering. She went to another room to prepare his body for burial.

Jonathan tried to stand up, but his left leg gave way beneath his weight. He grabbed the edge of the table, then swung around on his good leg, and sat down on a nearby chair. One of the neighbors brought a basin of water, and they washed Jonathan's leg and tightly wrapped a fresh cloth around it, trying to stop the flow of blood.

At the end of the day, Samuel and his family learned that Reuben was one of 6 babies killed by Herod's men. Six—the number of man and humanity. During the week of creation, Adam was created on the sixth day. The sixth commandment forbids murder. Six precious, innocent babies murdered by a Jewish man who wanted to retain his power and position as King of Israel.

The families in Bethlehem could not understand such a diabolical mindset, and they could not be comforted. Many years earlier, Jeremiah the prophet had prophesied this event when he said, "A voice is heard in Ramah, lamentation and bitter weeping, Rachel is weeping for her children; she refuses to be comforted for her children, because they are no more"[25] (Jeremiah 31:15).

In the ancient Jewish tradition, all of the babies killed by Herod's soldiers were buried the following day. Rueben's body was washed and wrapped in white cloth. The family walked to the community graveyard for the short ceremony. Because of their injuries, Jonathan and Rachel could hardly walk, so Samuel carried Reuben's little body and placed it in the hole that had been dug. Samuel spoke about Reuben and shared how his birth had brought such joy to their family. Samuel recited the famous Psalm written by King David years earlier.

"Psalm 23

> The Lord is my shepherd; I shall not want.
> He makes me lie down in green pastures.
> He leads me beside still waters.
> He restores my soul.
> He leads me in paths of righteousness for his name's sake.

---

[25] See prophecy 15 in Prophecy Chart.

Even though I walk through the valley of the shadow of death,
I will fear no evil, for you are with me.
Your rod and your staff, they comfort me.

You prepare a table before me, in the presence of my enemies.
You anoint my head with oil; my cup overflows.
Surely, goodness and mercy shall follow me all the days of my life,
And I shall dwell in the house of the Lord forever."
(Psalm 23:1–6)

At the end of the Psalm, Samuel recited an ancient prayer that mentioned the greatness of Adonai and that G-d would never leave them, even in times of great trouble. He spoke about the faithfulness of Adonai from one generation to the next, without end. Samuel understood his family was on a path no one wanted to walk, but he also knew G-d would walk with them on their journey of sorrow.

When Samuel finished speaking, one of their neighbors began to cover Rueben's body with the dirt. At the sound of the dirt hitting the small, white-draped body, Rachel buried her head in Jonathan's shoulder and wept. The family walked solemnly back to their home. After they entered their home, everyone washed their hands, and they lit a candle in remembrance of Reuben. Samuel and his family sat down at the table. Their neighbors provided a meal and would continue to do so for the next week. This would give Samuel and his family the proper time to grieve. No work would be done during this time of mourning; it was the way of the shepherds.

But everyone knew their lives would never be the same.

Thought Provoking Journey:

- When the innocent babies in Bethlehem were killed, what did the families in Bethlehem think and how did they feel? Did they blame God?

- Why does God allow bad things to happen to good people?

- Since the fall of man and the promise that the 'seed of the women', through a descendent of Abraham, Isaac and Jacob, would bruise the head of the serpent (the enemy of God, also known as Satan), evil people have tried to annihilate the Jewish people. In over 4,000 years of human history, no other people group has been so mistreated.

www.ngcarraway.com

Chapter 12 Thoughts

Chapter 13
Not 'til Then

◄·· ——————— ა◆ა ——————— ··►

Five years later...

It was the beginning of fall. Josiah sat on the hillside and looked down at the town of Bethlehem. He was now 17 years old. As he watched over the sheep, he reflected back on the past 7 years. He vividly remembered the very spot where the angels appeared and announced the birth of Yeshua. Each time he remembered, he felt a chill, and he knew unseen angels were nearby. Bethlehem experienced so much joy when the Messiah was born in their town. Samuel, now bent over and frail, walked over and sat down next to Josiah.

"I know what you are thinking," Samuel said while nodding his head. The wind gently blew his long beard, now gray from years of grief and struggle.

"You remember, don't you?" Pointing to a spot a few feet away, Samuel continued, "The angels, appeared over there. They told us the good news that a Savior had been born and he was the Messiah. We found him in the Tower of the Flock, wrapped in swaddling clothes and lying in a manger, just like they said."

"Yes, father, I remember, even though it was years ago. I wonder where Yeshua is now. He escaped the, the soldiers.... and, and the..." Josiah could not continue, and tears welled up in his eyes.

"Never forget, Josiah! When terrible things happen, never forget that G-d sent His son because we *need* a Savior."

"I, I know, father, but it is hard sometimes..." Josiah stammered. "Jonathan is, is crippled, and he cannot help with the sheep. I thought Rachel would have another baby after... after... Reuben... but I heard mother say Rachel would *never* be able to have a baby. When the solider kicked Rachel, mother said something happened.... I don't know what, but that is why Rachel bled so much..."

Josiah stared intently at his father as if looking for answers. "It's not fair! Jonathan and Rachel are good people! Why did this happen to them?" Josiah cried out.

"Josiah, listen to me! Bad things happen because of man's sin and man's evil heart. Each man has a choice to make, but it is *never* G-d's will for bad things to happen to good people. Remember the story of Job?"

Samuel placed his arm around Josiah and said, "One day, Josiah. Our Messiah *will* come with *authority*, and everything wrong will be made right. But not until then. Our hearts and souls yearn for that day. Remember; Adonai, our G-d never lies!"

That night, as the shepherds slept near their sheep, on the hillside overlooking Bethlehem, Josiah had another dream. The next morning, he grabbed his lyre and shouted for Samuel, "Father, come and listen. I had another dream last night. It's a song; I heard it in my dream."

Samuel sat next to Josiah as he began to strum the lyre and softly sing.

"As long as evil men have power, the innocent will die
It matters not the reason, or how they justify
It's a heart of hate that drives them, a spirit deep inside
That seeks to steal and kill and then destroy with jealous pride

When will this nightmare finish? When will this evil end?
When will the children laugh again? Oh please just tell me when

When our Messiah comes, with a scepter in His hand
With power and authority that no one can withstand
He will sit upon His throne and bring peace throughout the land
We will live in harmony, but not 'til then...

When will our Savior come, and when will men speak peace?
To each and every nation, when will our troubles cease?
When will our hearts be tender and full of gentleness?
When will our men and women long to live in holiness?
When will this dream of heaven, bring peace that has no end?
When will the people love again? Oh please just tell me when

When our Messiah comes, with a scepter in His hand
With power and authority that no one can withstand
He will sit upon His throne and bring peace throughout the land
We will live in harmony, but not 'til then..."

As Josiah sang this simple song, all of the shepherds gathered near him. Each man had lost someone dear, during the day of Herod's wrath; a son, a brother, a nephew, a friend. When Josiah finished singing, there was not a dry eye among them.

Samuel slowly stood up, patted Josiah on the shoulder, and said, "Keep dreaming, Josiah. And keep singing."

As he walked away, he said, "And *never* lose hope; our Messiah *will* come in power."

A few days later, Josiah and his father traveled back to their house while other shepherds watched their sheep. Samuel, Josiah, and Jonathan were planning to travel to Jerusalem for the Feast of

Tabernacles the following day. The next morning, after breakfast, the three men packed up and started on their trip.

"Jonathan, why don't you ride on the donkey instead of walking?" Samuel gently suggested.

Jonathan hung in head in shame and, with Josiah's help, he slowly mounted the donkey, dragging his wooden crutch behind him.

"I will only ride for a short time, and then Josiah can ride," Jonathan mumbled.

Samuel and Josiah both nodded their heads in agreement, but everyone knew Jonathan would ride on the donkey for the entire trip. They loaded a few belongings on the donkey's back and started down the path to Jerusalem.

It was not long before Samuel began his usual practice of teaching his sons while walking to Jerusalem. Samuel knew his sons could not be distracted by their normal tasks, and it helped to pass the time.

"Josiah, our rabbi recently taught on the prophecies in our holy scriptures about the coming Messiah," Samuel began. "I saw the confused look on your face when the rabbi said there might be two Messiahs."

"Yes! He did not explain *how* there could be *two* Messiahs," Josiah replied. "He called one Messiah 'the son of Joseph.' Was he talking about Yeshua, Mary's baby born at the Tower seven years ago? Her husband was called Joseph."

"No, he was not *really* referring to Joseph who lived here in Bethlehem with Mary and Yeshua. He was referring to Joseph, the son of Jacob, who became second in command under Pharaoh. You remember the story of how Joseph's brothers sold him into slavery, and he was taken to Egypt as a slave. But Joseph was a humble person whom G-d raised up to save the people from a terrible future famine."

"Our rabbis teach from the book of Zechariah about a future king for our people. The scriptures state: 'Behold, your king is coming to you; righteous and having salvation is he, humble and mounted on a donkey... and He will speak peace to the nations; his rule shall be from sea to sea.' These verses show this king does not ride a great horse or a chariot, but he comes riding on a lowly donkey. This king does not come with an army, but He still proclaims peace. This shows how meek and gentle this king will be" (Zechariah 9:9–10).

"This humble person is called **Messiah, son of Joseph** because Joseph was meek and gentle but rose to power in Egypt without an army. But there is *another* scripture in Zechariah which states: 'For I will gather all the nations against Jerusalem to battle, and the city will be taken... Then the LORD will go out and fight against those nations as when he fights on a day of battle (Zechariah 14:2–3). And the LORD will be king over all the earth. On that day the LORD will be the one, and his name one,' (Zechariah 14:9) Samuel explained.

"This person, the one who fights in battle is called **Messiah, son of David**. This is a reference to David, the shepherd boy who killed the wicked giant called Goliath. David was a mighty warrior and won many battles against his enemies after he became the King of Israel."

"I don't understand," Josiah confessed. "The scriptures contain prophecies about the future Messiah who will be our king. But how could there be two Messiahs?"

"Our rabbis continue to study the scriptures to try and understand this mystery. Some of the Essenes believe that the Messiah will be born and die and then be resurrected. Other people believe there will be two different men, who are two different Messiahs. You are betrothed to Abigail and her father is a rabbi. In a few years, when you get married, perhaps you can discuss these prophecies with him. But never forget, when the angels told us Yeshua was born, they told us he is our Messiah," Samuel reassured him.

"Well, I did not hear the angels announcement, like both of you did," Jonathan snapped. "If Yeshua *is* the Messiah, he should come as the son of David. We need a *warrior* king who can fight for us!"

Samuel squinted at his oldest son on the donkey. His eyes were like an arrow as he chastised Jonathan, "The Messiah will be who G-d made him to be, whether we understand it or not."

Jonathan scowled and mumbled under his breath, "It's time to fight for our families and our way of life."

Josiah glanced at his father and at Jonathan. These arguments were becoming a common occurrence between the two men he loved most. Of course, he knew his father was right. Ever since Herod's soldiers murdered Jonathan's son, Reuben, and Jonathan's leg was cut open by the soldier's sword, it was as if something was broken inside of Jonathan. His leg was so damaged that he was now crippled and walked with a crutch. His wife, Rachel, could no longer have children. When Herod's soldiers came to Bethlehem, Jonathan's future was completely shattered and broken. And deep down inside of Jonathan, he was broken too.

It was difficult for Josiah to see his brother this way. As they continued to walk toward Jerusalem, Josiah silently said a prayer for Jonathan and Rachel, a prayer only Adonai would hear and only Adonai could answer.

When they reached Jerusalem, they entered through the Essene Gate and found an inn for the night; they followed the familiar path to the Temple. Jonathan continued to ride the donkey up the hill until they reached the steps leading to the Temple complex. As they traveled, they passed many Roman soldiers who were arrogant and rude, pushing and shoving the Jewish men and women. Some Jews were even knocked to the ground, while the Romans sneered.

Samuel would help the person back up and whisper in their ear, "Don't lose hope, our Messiah will show himself soon." In response to Samuel's confident tone, the person would nod their head and say, "By G-d's hand, may it be," or something similar.

The wicked King Herod had died a few years ago, not long after the massacre of the innocent babies. Now, Herod's three sons were in charge of Jerusalem and Judea. Jerusalem was beginning to feel the strain of political upheaval. There was constant strife between the various religious groups, the Pharisees, the Sadducees, and the Essenes.

The Pharisees were the educated rabbis who lived throughout the land of Israel. They were teachers of the Torah in their local synagogue. The Pharisees were "men of the Word" and highly respected by the hardworking Jew, the "common man."

The Sadducees, on the other hand, were the elites. They were part of the wealthy, educated, aristocratic Jews and were closely connected to the Temple priests. While they claimed to be a religious group, they were more of a power-hungry political party. The Sadducees cooperated with the Roman rulers, and as a result, they were rewarded with a majority of the seats in Israel's highest legal court. This gave them great power. They worked closely with the Roman occupiers in order to keep the peace, which infuriated the local people.

The Essenes were the smallest of the three religious groups. The Essenes were scribes who lived a sparse life in the desert community of Qumran, near the Salt Sea. These scribes were known for their devotion to the Torah texts and the Jewish patriarchs. But they insisted on using a different religious calendar than the Pharisees, which put them at odds with the general population. The Essene calendar was a solar calendar, so they were sometimes called the Sons of Light. The Essenes followed a different group of priests who were descendants of Zadok, the high priest during King David and King Solomon. These Zadok priests, as they were sometimes called, prophesied the Levitical priesthood would disappear from the temple and the Jewish Temple would eventually be destroyed. Of course, this was not a popular prophecy with the Temple priests!

However, the true power in Jerusalem was the Roman government, and all of the religious parties were under the rule of the local Roman officials. The Roman soldiers were part of the most powerful military in the world, and everyone was forced to acknowledge their rule.

Once Samuel and his sons were inside the Temple complex, they decided to purchase a goat for a burnt offering, giving G-d the entire sacrifice as an offering. While they waited for the animal to be handed over, they overhead one of the Temple priests and one of the Sadducees talking to the man selling at the next booth.

"You know you must give us a part of the price," the priest argued.

The man in the booth crossed his arms and challenged, "What happens if I don't give you some of my profit?"

"You will *not* be allowed to sell on the Temple Mount," the Sadducee exclaimed furiously. He and the priest walked to a nearby Roman soldier. The Sadducee and the priest talked with the solider and pointed to the merchant. The solider nodded his head and put his hand on his sword. The man at the booth shook his head angrily and mumbled something to himself.

Samuel picked up the goat they had purchased. Jonathan then spoke up and said, "I am really tired. I think I will wait here while you offer the sacrifice."

Samuel nodded his head, turned to Josiah, and softly said, "Come, let us offer our goat to Adonai."

As they walked toward the gate of the Holy Temple, Josiah had a puzzled look on his face.

"Jonathan should come with us, he can't be that tired. He rode on the donkey all the way from Bethlehem," Josiah stated matter-of-factly.

"Josiah, I need to explain to you that Jonathan will never be able to come into the Holy Temple courtyard which is reserved for the Jewish people," Samuel said with great sadness. "Our rabbis believe that if a person is lame, blind, mute, or has certain diseases... our rabbis believe these people are unclean. They believe that the person's affliction is the result of sin in the person's life. The unclean people are not allowed into the Holy Temple area. Jonathan must stay outside, where the Gentiles, the unclean gather."

"Jonathan is not lame because of sin in his life!" Josiah quickly countered. "Herod's soldier's made him lame when they came and killed the babies in Bethlehem. The soldier struck Jonathan's leg with his sword. I saw it myself!"

"Yes, I know," Samuel replied. "Our rabbis also teach that when the Messiah comes, he will have the power to heal the lame, open the eyes of the blind and the ears of the mute, and even heal leprosy. One day, when our Messiah comes, with power and authority, he will do these miracles."

"Then, I will pray that Yeshua will heal Jonathan's leg," Josiah replied confidently.

"Yes, I pray that also," Samuel added.

Samuel and Josiah went through the Temple gate into the courtyard, where their sacrifice was offered. Then, they returned to where Jonathan was waiting with the merchants.

As they left the Temple Mount and returned to the donkey, Jonathan said in disgust, "The priests and Sadducees care only about the money they can extort from simple merchants."

"The Messiah will come and make everything right," replied Samuel.

"I am tired of hearing that one day the Messiah will come, and everything will be made right. The only way to make some things right is to fight against the evil men who control everything!" Jonathan ranted.

"Jonathan, the Messiah has come! He was born in Bethlehem! The angels told us where to find him. You *must* believe Adonai has spoken through His angels," Samuel said, encouraging him.

"I did *not* see the angels. All I know is Reuben is dead and I am half a man," Jonathan snarled.

"Adonai, our G-d, never lies; always remember that... G-d never lies. But Yeshua must grow up before he can be used by Adonai," Samuel exhorted.

"Yeshua would be seven years old now. I wonder where he is," Samuel said softly with a faraway look in his eyes.

Thought Provoking Journey:

- For thousands of years, Jewish scholars have debated the prophecies of a redeemer for their people, the anointed one called the Messiah.

- During the time of Herod's Temple, the Jewish people were looking for a military or a political leader to deliver them from Roman oppression, and then rule as their king.

- After the Jewish Holy Temple was destroyed in 70 AD, and the Jews were scattered throughout the world, some began to look for a personal Messiah to end their suffering and to bring them back to Israel.

- Traditional Judaism teaches there may be two Messiahs; Messiah, son of Joseph (the suffering servant) and Messiah, son of David (the conquering king).

- Are there other prophecies about Israel and the Jewish people which have not yet been fulfilled?

Chapter 13 Thoughts

Chapter 14
The Young Scholar

<... ———— ❦ ———— ...>

Samuel did not know that after leaving Bethlehem, Yeshua was living in Egypt with Mary and Joseph. After King Herod died, Joseph had a dream, and an angel appeared to him. The angel told Joseph that King Herod was dead and it was finally safe to return to Israel. Joseph took Mary and her son, Yeshua, and they headed toward Israel, thinking they would return to Bethlehem. But when he heard that Herod's son was now the ruler over Bethlehem, he was afraid to live there. Joseph had another dream, and G-d warned him to go farther north, to the area of Galilee. Therefore, Joseph took Mary and her son, Yeshua, to Nazareth. (Matthew 2:19).

Yeshua grew up in Nazareth; he became strong in spirit and he was filled with wisdom. It was evident that the hand of G-d was upon him (Luke 2:39–40).

Yeshua and his family observed the weekly Sabbath and the annual feasts, as required in the scriptures. Every year, Yeshua and his parents would travel to Jerusalem for Pesach (Passover). When Yeshua was twelve years old, they traveled to Jerusalem with relatives and friends, as was the custom. When the Passover feast was over, Mary and Joseph began to walk back to Nazareth, thinking Yeshua was with their relatives. However, Yeshua stayed behind in Jerusalem, without their knowledge.

At the end of the first day of travel, Mary and Joseph began to look for Yeshua, but they could not find him. They asked their relatives and friends, but no one had seen Yeshua since they left Jerusalem. Mary was frantic! Yeshua was missing, and she did not know where he was or what had happened. That night, Mary could hardly sleep, and she cried for a long time.

Joseph tried to comfort her. "Mary, we will find him. He must still be in Jerusalem. We will walk back to Jerusalem in the morning. He is probably at the inn where we stayed. I am sure the innkeeper is taking good care of him."

In the morning, they said goodbye to their relatives and friends. They explained they were traveling back to Jerusalem to search for Yeshua. The women hugged Mary and promised to pray and ask Adonai to guide their steps.

"I am sure Yeshua is okay; he is a good boy. And Adonai has protected him since he was born," Joseph reassured Mary.

"Yes, I know, Joseph, but he is so young. He is only twelve years old!" Mary groaned. "Where could Yeshua be? Jerusalem is such a big city. It is easy to get lost, even for an adult. He is all alone."

When they arrived back in Jerusalem, they headed to the inn where they stayed a couple of days earlier, but Yeshua was not there. Mary cried herself to sleep that night; she felt like this was her fault. As a mother, it was her responsibility to *always* know where her children were and to make sure they were safe.

After searching for three days, they decided to go to the Temple mount. To their amazement, Yeshua was sitting in the Temple courtyard with a group of rabbis. He was listening to their teaching and asking them questions. When Mary and Joseph saw Yeshua, Mary rushed to him, tears streaming down her face. She wrapped her arms around him and held him tightly.

"Son, why have you treated us like this? Your father and I have been anxiously searching for you!" Mary cried out.

One of the rabbis blurted out, "We were amazed at his questions but more amazed at his answers. For such a young boy, his understanding of the holy scriptures is well beyond his years."

Yeshua hugged his mother briefly, and then gently pulled away from her, holding both of her arms for emphasis. He looked directly into her eyes and asked, "Why were you searching for me? Didn't you know I had to be in my Father's house?"

Mary's mouth dropped open in shock. "His father's house?" she thought. His statement did not make sense to Mary; she did not understand *exactly* what Yeshua meant. For years now, when they met people, she identified Joseph as the father of Yeshua.

Joseph reached out to Yeshua and placed his arm around his shoulders. "Come with us, Yeshua," Joseph said sternly as he led Yeshua away from the rabbis. Mary was deeply relieved!

"His father's house, that's what he said," she thought. "He is twelve years old, and he knows he is the son of G-d! Adonai is starting to reveal himself to Yeshua." She was stunned! She remembered the angelic visitation and the birth of Yeshua. This day would be another memory that she would keep in her heart, as she treasured all of these precious memories.

The family returned to Nazareth, and Yeshua was obedient to his parents. Yeshua continued to grow in wisdom and stature. Because of his excellent character and his knowledge of the Holy Scriptures, he found favor with men, and more importantly, he found favor with G-d. (Luke 2:41–52)

Thought Provoking Journey:

- In the Jewish tradition, by the age of twelve, boys have learned right and wrong from the Torah, and they are now accountable for their decisions and actions.

- There are no scriptures, in the Bible, which describe Yeshua's childhood, other than the story when he is twelve years old in the Temple.

- Bible scholars believe that Yeshua (Jesus) was taught to obey the Torah commandments, to observe the Sabbath and to celebrate the seven annual feasts which God ordained in Leviticus. As such, each year, he would have traveled to Jerusalem for the three required pilgrimage feasts (Passover, Pentecost and Tabernacles). Each feast had a hidden prophetic meaning; Passover foreshadowed the crucifixion of Jesus. Pentecost foreshadowed the outpouring of the Holy Spirit on His disciples. Tabernacles foreshadows a time when God will live in the midst of his people.

- What do the other feasts foreshadow?

www.ngcarraway.com

Chapter 14 Thoughts

Chapter 15
Golden Glow of Glory

"Josiah, come quickly; I need you!" Abigail shouted from the window. Josiah ran into the house and saw his wife holding her stomach. "I think the baby is coming, get the midwife," Abigail begged.

"Okay, I'll get mother too!" Josiah shouted as he ran to the back of the house to get his mother. He then bolted out the door in search of the midwife and his sister Hannah, who lived down the street.

Josiah and his wife lived in the same house with his parents, Jonathan, and Rachel. Before he and Abigail got married, two years ago, he added a room onto his father's house.

Josiah was now 22 years old and the main provider for his entire family. Jonathan was no longer able to walk the rocky hills to tend the sheep. Nevertheless, he would help with the sheep when they were kept in the town's sheep pen. A few years earlier, Samuel had lost the strength in his left arm and hand; no one knew what caused his condition. He helped as much as he could, but he was becoming weak and frail.

When Josiah returned home with the midwife, the men were in the front room, and the women were in the bedroom with Abigail. The midwife quickly told the women what to do, and she made Josiah leave the room.

Josiah joined the men but could not sit still. He paced back and forth. Every time he heard Abigail's muffled scream, he glanced toward the room. After several hours of nervous anxiety, he finally heard the sound of a baby crying.

The midwife came out and announced, "Josiah, you have a healthy baby boy. And Abigail is doing great. Give her a few minutes, and then you can go see them both."

Josiah breathed a sigh of relief as the men shouted, "A boy; praise G-d!"

A few minutes later, Josiah went to check on Abigail. When he came out, he carried a tiny baby, wrapped in soft cloth. Josiah sat down between Jonathan and Samuel. Everyone stared at the little baby, who stared back at them with dark eyes. The men talked about his tiny hands, his dark hair, and his strong legs pushing against the cloth.

"Have you decided on a name?" Samuel asked.

"Yes," answered Josiah. He looked at Jonathan and said, "We have decided to name him Reuben." He handed the baby to Jonathan, who slowly took the bundle in his lap while tears began to flow down his face.

"If that's all right with you, Jonathan," Josiah quickly added.

"Yes, yes, that is okay with me. Thank you," Jonathan softly mumbled. Jonathan gently touched Reuben's tiny hand with his finger. Unexpectedly, Reuben clenched Jonathan's finger and would not let go. The men all laughed.

"I think Reuben likes his uncle Jonathan," Josiah exclaimed. "I need to take him back to Abigail now."

Josiah slowly removed Reuben's hand from Jonathan's finger and took Reuben back to Abigail.

Jonathan also left the room. He hobbled back to the room he shared with Rachel, wiping tears from his eyes with his free hand. In a few minutes, Josiah came back and sat next to his father.

"Father, when I was in Jerusalem yesterday, I heard a conversation at the Temple. They were talking about a young boy," Josiah blurted out. "I have been meaning to tell you what I heard, I forget when I got home, and Abigail was in labor."

"What did they say?" inquired Samuel.

"An old rabbi was telling a group of his friends that after Passover, a young boy walked up to a group of rabbis, while they were in Solomon's Portico, on the Temple mount, discussing the Torah. This young boy began to ask the rabbis questions about the scriptures. The rabbis were amazed at his questions which they said were well beyond his years. They thought he was about twelve years old."

"Really?" Samuel asked. "Maybe he is from a family of rabbis? Did they say what his name was?"

"The old rabbi said his name was Yeshua; the boy did not mention any rabbis in his family. Do you think he was Yeshua who was born here in Bethlehem twelve years ago?" Josiah asked excitedly.

"The name Yeshua has been a very common name to give boys for decades now, especially among the Essenes. There must be hundreds or thousands of boys with that name," Samuel explained.

"But what if he is Yeshua, the Messiah?" Josiah proposed.

"Did the rabbis say anything else about this boy?" Samuel countered.

"Yes, they said he came back to the Temple for three days. Every day, they were more amazed at his questions and answers. He asked them many questions about the prophecies concerning the Messiah. They said his understanding was profound; they could not believe what they were hearing," Josiah replied.

"On the third day of discussions, a man and his wife came to the Temple. They said he was their son and they had been looking for him. They left to travel back to their home, taking the boy with them."

"Did they say where this family lived?" Samuel asked.

"No, they did not know much more about him. But they could not stop talking about his knowledge of the scriptures and the questions he asked. Sometimes, even these learned rabbis did not know how to answer him."

Samuel closed his eyes and softly said, "More than twelve years ago, Yeshua, our Messiah, was born. I am sure his parents will teach him the Torah. And I am sure G-d will lead him in paths of righteousness. And, when he is older, he will be a teacher of righteousness."

Samuel opened his eyes and stared intently at Josiah. "Maybe he *is* our Messiah! You must always be looking for Yeshua. We do not know *when* he will reveal himself, or *how* he will do this. Somehow, when he is older, he *will* reveal himself to our people. He may even be a rabbi explaining the scriptures which have been written about himself."

"Josiah, you need to search the scriptures and study the prophecies about our Messiah. We already know some prophecies were fulfilled when Yeshua was born here, in Bethlehem. However, there are many more prophecies about the work that the Messiah will do. Study the scriptures so you will recognize the Messiah when he appears."

"Yes, father, I have already begun to study the scriptures. Abigail's father let me borrow his scroll. I am memorizing the prophecies which I find, even if I don't understand them," Josiah replied as he stood up.

"And I will teach Reuben about the prophecies too," Josiah said as he walked back to the room where his newborn boy now slept.

A few months later, Josiah had a dream about his father. It had been a long time since he had dreamed. In this dream, his father was walking through a field of wheat toward a city in the distance. As he walked, his hands touched the tops of the golden grains of wheat. His father was young, strong, and healthy, and his hair and beard were brown. The distant city emanated a golden glow, and the entire sky above the wheat glistened with the same glow. After walking a few feet, Samuel turned around, smiled, and waved his hand for people to follow him. He continued walking, in the glorious golden glow, toward the beautiful city ahead. Jonathan woke up.

He was stunned by what he saw in his dream! "What does it mean?" he wondered. The place where his father walked was perfectly peaceful and beautiful. Even more beautiful than Jerusalem! It seemed as if the very air had a golden, radiant shimmer. And his father was young and strong. He knew he would never forget that dream, but he told no one about it.

A few days later, Josiah was checking on his sheep in the town's local pen, where they stayed for winter. The weather had turned cold the day before, and there was even ice on the top of the water buckets. Suddenly, Josiah heard the voice of Jonathan calling him. He turned around to see Jonathan hobbling down the street.

"Josiah, hurry, it is father! He fell, something is wrong!" Jonathan shouted.

Josiah ran toward the home they all shared. When he entered, he saw his father lying on the floor. His mother was shaking him and saying, "Get up, Samuel, please get up!"

Josiah helped his father get up from the floor, but his movements were awkward and stiff. With the help of his mother and Jonathan, they were able to get Samuel to a chair. Samuel looked dazed as he glanced around the room at the members of his family, who now surrounded him.

Samuel could not move his left arm or his left leg. He was struggling to breathe. He looked at Josiah with great intensity in his eyes and grabbed Josiah's robe with his right hand, pulling him closer.

"Josiah, Adonai our G-d never lies! His word is true! You saw the angels and you saw Yeshua, the Messiah. Promise me you will *never* forget, that you will always remember that night!" Samuel implored.

"Yes, father, I promise!" Josiah replied, tears streaming down his face.

"And promise that you will search for him! If you search for him, you will find him!" Samuel exhorted. "You had an encounter with Yeshua when he was born. But you need to have another encounter, after he becomes an adult. Then, you will *not* deny his existence nor his authority. Remember the prophecies; those are the clues to finding him."

"Yes, I promise!" Josiah stated emphatically.

With labored breath, Samuel said, "You will know that a man named Yeshua *is the Messiah* when he begins to fulfill the prophecies which have been spoken about him. That will be the proof that G-d has anointed him as our Messiah. Only G-d could speak prophecies hundreds of years ago and cause them to be fulfilled in one man, in our day. That is the evidence, that is the proof the world needs," Samuel assured his family.

Samuel let out a long breath and closed his eyes. His hand dropped from Josiah's robe and Samuel died.

A few hours later, the sun set; it was a beautiful, golden, pink sunset. Everyone remarked at what a glorious sunset appeared on the day that Samuel died. Josiah called it "the golden glow of glory." Josiah realized the dream he had a few days earlier was to let him know his father would soon be passing from this world to paradise and to the glorious world of eternal life.

Bethlehem sunset

The funeral was the following day, in the same cemetery where Rueben had been buried, years earlier. Josiah helped his mother walk as she leaned heavily on his arm. After the body was placed in the ground and covered with dirt, Josiah said a prayer:

"Blessed are you, O Lord, our G-d. You sustain the living with lovingkindness. And you fulfill your faithfulness to those who sleep in the ground. You are trustworthy to revive the dead. May your will be done in heaven above. Grant peace of mind to those who fear you on the earth below. Who is like you, King of the Universe? Holy is the Lord of Hosts, the entire world is filled with His glory. Blessed be the name of His glorious kingdom forever."

As Josiah prayed, it began to snow. He looked up into the sky in amazement. He had never seen snow before. Josiah was stunned that he saw snow, for the first time, at his father's funeral. He remembered when he saw hail the first time. His father told him it was a mystery, that hail was another form of water. After the prayer, the family returned home and began the traditional time of mourning. Samuel had been a spiritual leader in Bethlehem, and the entire town mourned with Josiah's family.

Over the next few days, Josiah thought about the mystery of hail and snow, which both fall from the sky, like the rain. But they are not rain, simply other forms of water. He remembered a teaching from his rabbi about humanity and how we are made of three parts; spirit, soul, and body.

One day, he went to the Tower of the Flock and thought of Yeshua and all of the prophecies about the Messiah. Yeshua was the son of G-d, the Messiah, born of a virgin. He slowly realized that the creator of the Universe *could* create a baby in Mary's womb, a baby who was *another* form of G-d. The Scriptures also speak of the *Holy Spirit* as the spirit of G-d, *another* form of G-d. In Psalm 51:11, David wrote, "Cast me not away from your presence, and take not your Holy Spirit from me."

Josiah recited the first part of the Shema prayer, "Hear O Israel, the Lord our G-d, the Lord is one!" And the unfolding of the mystery of G-d began to take place in his mind. There is only one G-d. But three in one! G-d in heaven, his Spirit on earth, and His son Yeshua, now living on the earth; three different forms, but one G-d!

Josiah felt a supernatural peace come over his body and his mind. He promised his father that he would never forget that the Messiah had already been born. He reflected on the prophecies that were fulfilled when Yeshua was born, the night he saw the angels, more than 12 years ago. One by one, he remembered the ancient prophecies he knew had been fulfilled. Maybe there were more that he was not aware of.

1. The Messiah would be the seed of the woman.
2. The Messiah would be born in Bethlehem.
3. The Messiah would be a descendant of David.
4. The Messiah would be the descendant of Abraham through whom all nations would be blessed.
5. The Messiah would be the coming one to whom the scepter belongs (a descendent of Judah).
6. The Messiah would be called God's son.
7. The Messiah would be the star coming out of Jacob.
8. There would be weeping in Bethlehem.

Josiah remembered the song in his dream about the Messiah. As he sat in the tower, by the stone manger where Yeshua had slept, he began to strum his lyre and sing part of the song:

> When our Messiah comes, with a scepter in His hand
> With power and authority that no one can withstand
> He will sit upon His throne and bring peace throughout the land
> We will live in harmony, but not 'til then...[26]

---

[26] An audio of the song "When Our Messiah Comes" is available on the author's website (ngcarraway.com).

Josiah reflected that he might wait years before he heard anything about Yeshua, the Messiah born in Bethlehem. But Josiah knew that no matter what happened to him or his family, or even his nation, the Messiah *would* come one day. Because Adonai, our G-d, never lies.

To be continued...

Journey on the Ancient Path - The Way of the Shepherd
Chapter 15 - The Golden Glow of Glory

Thought Provoking Journey:

- The Hebrew word for sky, or heaven, is 'shamayim' and its form is plural. Why is this a plural word? Maybe it is because there are three different heavens? The scriptures mention the first heaven (which is the earthly sky), the second heaven (which is the natural, outer space) and the third heaven (where God lives).

- When Yeshua (Jesus) was born, he fulfilled every prophecy in the Tanakh (the Old Testament), concerning the birth of the Jewish Messiah.

- How many other ancient prophecies did Jesus fulfill when he became an adult?

- Yeshua (Jesus) is the most famous Jew that has ever lived.

- The Christian religion is a mono-theistic religion, which means a belief in only one supreme God who is omnipotent, omnipresent and omniscient.

- When Yeshua was born, he literally split time in half. The calendar we use today is divided into the years before Jesus was born and the years after he was born.

Chapter 15 Thoughts

Now What?

After you finish reading this book, you may still have questions about this account of the birth and life of Yeshua, Jesus Christ. The family of Josiah is a fictional family, but based on the shepherds who lived in Bethlehem, when Jesus was born. The scriptural account of this birth can be found in the Holy Bible. No one really knows the date of Jesus' birth or where his birth actually took place. Some scholars think that Jesus was born in the spring, others think he was born in the winter. Some scholars believe Jesus was born in a cave near Bethlehem. So, this account of Jesus is hypothetical, but based on scriptures concerning John the Baptist and the Tower of the Flock. We only know that Jesus was born in Bethlehem and placed in a manger.

If you are not familiar with the Holy Bible, it is best described as a collection of over sixty books, written by forty different authors under the inspiration of God, and written over a span of more than a thousand years. The first books were written around 1,500 BC and the last book was written around 95AD. This collection of books is divided into two sections, normally called the Old Testament and the New Testament. The Old Testament is considered the Hebrew Bible or the Jewish Tanakh. The first four books of the New Testament (Matthew, Mark, Luke and John), contain the account of the birth and life of Jesus. These four books are also called the Gospel, which means "good news".

The overall theme of the Holy Bible is that God, the One who created you, wants you to know Him and have a relationship with Him, but God does not condone a life of sin. Jesus, the son of God, lived a perfect life and died as the sacrifice for *your* sin, so that you can have a relationship with God the Father. You can be saved from a life of sin; after all, His name means "salvation"! After Jesus rose from the dead and ascended into heaven, he gave his disciples instructions to continue his ministry. In the book of Acts, when the first message was preached by the disciples of Jesus, the crowd asked what they should do, to be saved. Peter, one of the disciplines said, "Repent and be baptized every one of you in the name of Jesus Christ for the forgiveness of your sins, and you will receive the gift of the Holy Spirit. For the promise is for you and for your children and for all who are far off, everyone whom the Lord our God calls to himself." (Act 2:38-40)

Peter explained that the Holy Spirit was given to believers as a free gift. The Holy Spirit will lead you, and help you to live a life which is pleasing to God. When you are in a relationship with God, you should love what He loves and hate what He hates, and desire to live a life which is pleasing to him. This means you must study His Word, the Holy Bible, to understand the heart of God.

If you have never read the Holy Bible, and would like to start, I recommend that you begin with the Gospels. If you have a smart phone, one of the Bible apps can be downloaded free, in different languages. Most apps will allow you to toggle to different versions of the Holy Bible. I recommend the English Standard Version (ESV) or the New International Version (NIV). The website https://www.biblegateway. com is also a great resource with numerous versions of the Holy Bible.

If you still have questions about how to know the God of the Bible, you may read additional information which the author has posted on her website:

https://ngcarraway.com

The website listed below, and many other websites, can also answer your questions:

https://www.bibleinfo.com/en/questions/how-become-christian

Check the author's website for additional teaching and links to other Christian ministries and organizations.

Recommended Books and Websites

If you were raised in a **Jewish** culture:

- I recommend the book called "They Thought for Themselves: Ten Amazing Jews" by Sid Roth.
- The website https://www.oneforisrael.org also has helpful information. They have a YouTube channel called One For Israel, with numerous videos containing personal testimonies.
- The website https://jewsforjesus.org/100-percent offers a chat option and staff who will answer your questions.
- The website https://www.bethisraelworshipcenter.org is a website for a Messianic congregation in Wayne, New Jersey, USA where Rabbi Jonathan Cahn is the leader.

If you were raised in a **Muslim** culture, I recommend the book called "Seeking Allah, Finding Jesus: A Devout Muslim Encounters Christianity" by Nabeel Qureshi and Lee Strobel.

If you were raised in a **Hindu** culture, I recommend the book called "Death of a Guru" by Rabi R. Maharaj.

If you were raised in America, or in a **Christian** culture, you may think that you are already a Christian. But, if you have not been transformed by the Word of God, and the Spirit of God, are you truly saved? Ask yourself these questions:

- Have I ever truly repented for my sins and been transformed by God's grace?
- To repent means to turn around and go in the opposite direction. Has my life style changed since I repented?
- Have I received the free gift of the Holy Spirit?
- Does the Holy Spirit lead me and convict me when I begin to sin or stray from the truth?
- Do I have a hunger to know more about God and how He wants me to live?
- Do I know what God hates and what He calls sin?
- Do I desire to read His word, the Holy Bible, to learn more about God?
- Do I have a desire to meet with other believers for fellowship?
- Do I have a desire to share my faith with others?
- Am I a *disciple* of Jesus, a follower of His teachings?

Regardless of the culture within which you were raised, your heavenly Father loves you and has a plan for your life. Today is the day of salvation.

The first and greatest commandment is to love God with all your heart, with all your mind and with all your strength. But, the second greatest commandment is to **"Love your neighbor as yourself"**. May we all return to the feet of Jesus and study His teachings. And may we put into practice what Jesus taught and may we become more like Him!

When our Messiah comes, with power and authority, He will sit upon HIs throne and bring peace throughout the land. And we will live in harmony, but not 'til then.

Come quickly, Lord Jesus!

May the grace of the Lord Jesus be with you.

Journey on the Ancient Path - The Way of the Shepherd

NO.	Prophecies About The Birth Of The Messiah	Where Fulfilled In The New Testament
1	The Messiah would be the offspring (the seed) of a woman. (Genesis 3:15)	Luke 1:26-38, Luke 2:1-7
2	The Messiah would be born in Bethlehem. (Micah 5:2)	Matthew 2:1-6, Luke 2:1-7
3	God would send Elijah, the prophet, before the great and awesome 'Day of the Lord' comes. (Malachi 4:5)	Luke 1:5-25, Luke 1:57-79, Luke 3:1-6
4	The Messiah would be preceded by a forerunner. (Isaiah 40:3-5)	Matthew 3:1-3, Luke 3:1-6, John 1:22-23
5	The Messiah's birth would take place near the watch tower of the flock, in Bethlehem. (Micah 4:8)	Luke 2:4-7
6	The Messiah would be a descendant of David. (Isaiah 9:6-7, 2 Samuel 7:12-13)	Matthew 1:1-16, Luke 3:23-38
7	The Messiah would be a descendant of Abraham, through whom all nations would be blessed. (Genesis 12:3)	Matthew 1:1-16, Luke 3:23-38
8	The Messiah would be born 70 generations after Enoch. (Ancient texts in the Dead Sea Scrolls)	Luke 3:23-38
9	The Messiah would be born of the tribe of Judah, son of Jacob. (Genesis 49:10)	Matthew 1:1-16, Luke 3:23-33
10	The Messiah will reign on David's throne and over his kingdom. (Isaiah 9:7)	Luke 1:26-33
11	The Messiah would be born of a virgin. (Isaiah 7:14)	Matthew 1:22-23, Luke 1:30-37
12	The Messiah would be called God's son. (Psalm 2:7)	Luke 1:35, Mark 1:11
13	The Messiah would be the star coming out of Jacob (son of Isaac). (Numbers 24:17)	Matthew 2:2-6
14	The Messiah would be called out of Egypt. (Hosea 11:1)	Matthew 2:13-15
15	There would be weeping in Bethlehem (also known as Ramah) for the children. (Jeremiah 31:15)	Matthew 2:16-18

www.ngcarraway.com

Prophecy Chart

One New Man Menorah

Glossary	
Abraham - He lived around 1800 BCE.	Abraham was the man, chosen by G-d, with whom to make an eternal covenant; a covenant between the G-d of the universe and Abraham and his descendants.
Adam and Eve	Adam was the first man and Eve was the first woman created by G-d. He placed them in the Garden of Eden, which was perfect. When they disobeyed G-d, they were forced to leave the Garden. All human beings are descendants of Adam and Eve.
Adonai - Another name for the G-d of the Bible	In Judaism, the name of G-d is so holy that is cannot be spoken. The word, Adonai, means 'Lord' and is often used as a substitute for G-d. Adonai refers to the one and only G-d who created the heavens and the earth and is the King of the universe.
Ark of the Covenant	This was a wooden chest covered completely with gold (inside and out) and it contained the Ten Commandments and a couple of other holy artifacts. The Ark was placed in the Holy of Holies, inside the Holy Temple until it disappeared around 600 BCE. The presence of G-d rested on top of the Ark.
Chuppah	A canopy made of fabric and used during Jewish weddings and betrothals. The bride and groom stand under the canopy, which represents heaven.
Elijah - He lived around 900 BCE.	One of the most famous Jewish prophets of the Old Testament. He defended the worship of G-d, over the worship of Baal.
Ephod	A piece of garment worn by the High Priest; it was similar to an apron and worn over his robe. The front of the ephod contained a breastplate with 12 semi-precious stones. Each stone represented one of the 12 tribes of Israel.
Essenes	The Essenes were a religious group in Israel over 2,000 years ago. They lived a righteous lifestyle and believed the Zadok priestly lineage to be the true priests of Adonai.
Gentile	Any person, who is not Jewish by birth, is considered a Gentile.
G-d (God)	The G-d of the Bible and the creator of the universe and everything in it. G-d is omnipresent, omnipotent and omniscient.
Holy Bible	A collection of over sixty books, written by forty different authors, and written during a span of over a thousand years. The Bible is divided into two sections, commonly called the Old Testament and the New Testament by Christians. The Old Testament is used by the Jews and is called the Hebrew Scriptures, or the Tanakh, by them. The New Testament contains the account of the birth, life and ministry of Jesus and other writings by His disciples.
Holy Temple	Over 2,000 years ago, the Holy Temple was located on a small mount in the city of Jerusalem. It was the most holy place in Judaism and it was where animal sacrifices were made, as ordained by G-d. Over 1,000 priests normally served at the Temple in various duties.
Jewish Calendar	The lunar calendar currently used by the Jewish people. There is a civil calendar that begins in the fall and a religious calendar that begins in the spring. The seven Jewish feasts are based on the religious calendar.
Ketubah	An ancient Jewish contract between two families and their children, who are pledged to each other in marriage. It was a binding legal document.

Glossary–page 1

King David - He live around 1000 BCE.	David was a shepherd boy who lived in Bethlehem. He became famous for killing the giant Goliath, who was an enemy of Israel. Later, David became the King of Israel. He was also a musician and a poet and was the father of King Solomon. It was prophesied that the coming Messiah would be a descendent of David.
King Herod	An evil king who ruled Israel over 2,000 years ago, during the renovation of the Jewish Holy Temple (it was sometimes called Herod's Temple).
Levites	One of the twelve tribes of the Jewish people who descended from Abraham, Isaac and Jacob. All priests who served in the Holy Temple were required to be from the tribe of Levi and their descendants were called Levites.
Messiah	The Hebrew word translated as 'Messiah' means an 'anointed one', a person anointed or empowered for a specific task. In ancient Judaism, a future Messiah was promised through the lineage of Abraham and King David. The Jewish Messiah would defeat evil, save the people of Israel and bring peace to the world.
Moses - He lived around 1300 BCE.	Moses, also known as Moshe, is the most important prophet of Judaism. He led the children of Israel (about 3 million people) out of slavery in Egypt, where they had lived for 400 years. Moses led them to Mt. Sinai where G-d gave Moses the Ten Commandments, written on stone. Moses wrote the first five books of the Bible, called the Torah (or the Law).
Most High	A title used for the G-d of the Holy Bible, the G-d who is higher than any other god.
Pesach (Passover)	One of the three main feasts in Judaism. During ancient times in Israel, all Jewish men were required to travel to the Holy Temple, in Jerusalem, for this feast. This feast occurs in the spring and is called Passover by Christians. This feast has been celebrated for over 3,000 years.
Pharisees	The Pharisees where successful businessmen and leaders of the Jewish people 2,000 years ago. They were an influential religious (and sometimes political) sect within ancient Judaism. They tried to force others to follow their beliefs and rules. They believed in the supernatural, such as miracles and the resurrection of the dead.
Sabbath	The Sabbath is considered a Jewish holy day. It is also called Saturday, but it begins on Friday night at sundown and lasts until sundown on Saturday.
Sadducees	The Sadducees were Jewish aristocrats in Israel, over 2,000 years ago, and had legal and philosophical power. But, they were not deeply religious and rejected the supernatural elements of Judaism (angels, demons, miracles, the resurrection, etc.).
Shavuot (Pentecost)	One of the three main feasts in Judaism. It took place 7 weeks after Passover and was also called the Feast of Weeks. During ancient times in Israel, all Jewish men were required to travel to the Holy Temple, in Jerusalem, for this feast. This feast occurs in early summer and is called Pentecost by Christians.
Sukakh	A temporary three-sided shelter, built and used, during the Feast of Tabernacles.

Glossary–page 2

165

Shema Prayer	This prayer is the best-known Jewish prayer and has been recited for over 3,000 years. It is the most essential element of the Jewish faith. The prayer is considered the Greatest Commandment for Jews. The Jewish Shema prayer is spoken twice a day: "Shema Yisrael, Adonai Eloheinu, Adonai Echad. V'ahavta et Adonai Eloheicha b'chol l'vavcha u'vchol nafshcha uvechol modecha", which means "Hear O Israel: The Lord our G-d, the Lord is one. You shall love the Lord your G-d with all your heart, and with all your soul, and with all your might." (Deu 6:4-5)
Sukkot (Tabernacles)	One of the three main feasts in Judaism. During ancient times in Israel, all Jewish men were required to travel to the Holy Temple, in Jerusalem, for this feast. This is a seven day feast which occurs in early fall.
Synagogue	A Jewish place for worship and teaching, similar to a church.
Tanakh	The first half of the Bible; Christians call this the Old Testament. But, the appropriate word for the Hebrew scriptures is Tanakh. This word is an acronym for the three divisions of the Hebrew scriptures: Torah (the first 5 books), Nevi'im (Prophets) and Ketuvim (Writings).
Temple Mount	Another name for the mount on which the Jewish Holy Temple stood until 70 AD. While it stood, the Holy Temple was the center of Jewish worship. The Temple Mount also contained a large plaza with other buildings and was enclosed by a huge retaining wall. Part of this wall still stands today in Jerusalem; it is called the Western Wall (or Wailing Wall) and is a holy place for Jewish people.
Ten Commandments	Ten instructions (commandments) for how to live a holy life pleasing to G-d; these commandments are central to the teaching of Judaism and Christianity.
Torah	The first five books of the Bible (Genesis, Exodus, Leviticus, Numbers & Deuteronomy).
YHVH	The four Hebrew consonants yod, hey, vav, hey spell the holy name of G-d. The English equivalent is YHVH. In the Jewish tradition, the name of G-d is so holy that it cannot be spoken by anyone except the High Priest and then only at certain times during Temple services. But, since the Temple was destroyed in 70 AD, the holy name of G-d has not been spoken and the pronunciation has been lost.
Yom Kippur	The holiest day in Judaism, also called the Day of Atonement; it has been observed for over 3,000 years.
Yehovah (Jehovah)	The name of G-d in Hebrew is spelled with only the letters yod-hey-vav-hey. (YHVH). This name was translated as Yehovah by people who inserted the vowels they thought were correct. This was later translated (incorrectly) into Jehovah.
Zadok	The High Priest during King David's reign. His descendants were the only ones allowed to enter into the Holy Temple and offer incense to G-d.

Glossary–page 3

About the Author

N. G. (Gail) Carraway has been a lifelong student of the Holy
Bible and a lover of the God of creation and King of the universe. Gail was raised in a Christian home and grew up hearing the
ancient Biblical accounts of people like Moses, Joseph, Esther and
Noah. At a young age, Gail came to faith in Jesus (Yeshua) as the Son
of God, the Messiah of Israel and the Savior of the world.

A few years ago, in order to comprehend the mysteries hidden
within the Hebrew scriptures in the Tanakh (Old Testament), Gail
began to learn Hebrew. With this, her first book, she presents an
enthralling account of the birth of Yeshua (Jesus), the Messiah, from
a Jewish perspective.

For years, the Jewish feasts have been of particular interest to
Gail. While she is not a Biblical scholar, she understands that most
Christians have no knowledge of these feasts or the Jewish roots of the
Christian faith. With this book, Gail endeavors to educate others of
the symbolic meaning, and prophetic implication, of these feasts. Gail
has relied on her years of personal research, as well as inspiration from
the Holy Spirit, to explain the Jewish feasts and how they relate to us
and the times within which we live.

For those individuals who are not familiar with the amazing
account of the birth of Jesus (probably the most famous person who
has *ever* lived), this novel provides a realistic perspective of his birth,

based on the scriptures, but seen through the eyes of a fictional family of shepherds, who lived in Bethlehem.

Gail has a desire for you to have an *encounter* with the God of the Bible, not just a knowledge of the scripture of God. Her prayer is that this book will convey the extravagant love the heavenly Father has for you, His creation, and His Everlasting covenant with those who put their faith in Him. If you have a desire for a deeper understanding of God, come join the journey; there is always more to learn! Shalom and God bless!

Additional information and teaching can be found at:
Website: https://ngcarraway.com
Email: info@ngcarraway.com